SHADOW OF HEAVEN

I see the blue, the green, the golden and the red,
I have forgotten all the angel said.

The flower, the leaf, the meadow and the tree,
but of the words I have no memory.

KATHLEEN RAINE, 'ANGELUS'

...what if Earth

Be but the shadow of Heaven, and things therein

Each to other like more than on Earth is thought!

JOHN MILTON, PARADISE LOST

SCOTLAND

SHADOW OF HEAVEN

PATRICIA MACDONALD

with Angus Macdonald, pilot

With an Essay by Dominic Cooper

RIZZOLI
NEW YORK

For Mazoura Morrow Scott and Walter Scott

The publishers are grateful to the following for permission to reproduce
copyright material: Chatto & Windus Ltd for extracts from
Collected Poems and *Voice Over* by Norman MacCaig;
John Donald Publishers Ltd for an extract from *The Making of
the Crofting Community* by James Hunter; Faber & Faber Ltd and
Oxford University Press Inc., New York for extracts from *The Collected
Poems of Edwin Muir* by Edwin Muir (Copyright © 1960 by Willa Muir);
Macmillan Ltd, London and Basingstoke, for an extract from
Experimenting with An Amen by R.S. Thomas; Robin Munro for an
extract from *Poems of the Scottish Hills*; Kathleen Raine for an extract
from *Collected Poems*.

Half-title page photograph (p. 1):
Bend in the River Tweed near Bemersyde, Borders, 1987
Title page photograph (pp. 2-3):
Clouds and islands, Loch Lomond, 1985

First published in the United States of America in 1989 by
Rizzoli International Publications, Inc.
300 Park Avenue South, New York, NY 10010

Photographs and notes copyright © 1989 by Patricia Macdonald
Essay copyright © 1989 by Dominic Cooper

ISBN 0-8478-1093-3
LC 89 42688

Typeset by Spectrum Typesetting Limited, London
Printed and bound in Italy by L.E.G.O., Vicenza

CONTENTS

AN ESSAY BY DOMINIC COOPER

The open places: a few notes from West Ardnamurchan

Wind, stroking, carries seed and sea-smell before it; puffing, it rolls the lightness of loose things an inch or a mile, dust and pebble, briar and twig, to settle them anew. Bright days of its bounding work even surer deeds, whipping and whittling and boring in everywhere, forever tugging and easing half-strong things to weakness till they hang ready for the taking. Then the storm winds come, so much part of the days of darkness, with their streaming strength and vast walls of weight, ripping, crushing and driving up till the air becomes thick with a craze of branch shatter and flying grass from the hill.

Still now wind slices stone and rubs down the shape of things, much as it sliced and rubbed twenty-five thousand million moons ago in Archaeozoic times. Rain too has always been here, washing and polishing and jetting into rock on the back of storms; rain which, in these northern, drought-free parts, we love to curse, yet without which neither life nor even soil nor plant could ever have been. We dream back, yet it is almost beyond our comprehending, the scale of the first, life-founding rains. Before them, before all, the original wilderness was truly a dark, impossible place: fire-hot rock and unbroken night and giant winds moving beneath a canopy of impenetrable cloud. At last, with the cooling crust, the momentous downpour began, at first in blank darkness but later, as the cloud-cover thinned, through long nights and weakly illumined days: seamless rain that lasted five, maybe ten centuries, on and relentlessly on — until that miracle of days when the grey dome finally split and the sun first shone down on the enormous brightness of the collected rainwater that was now the sea. And so it was that there in the warm swell of the primal sea, the quiet alchemies spawned weed and worm, our early forefathers.

Ice and snow cramping tight have been the forces too, the slow roaming of the ice sheets in the centuries of cold bringing down earlier heights of upheaval, making turtleback and cupping of what before had been merely jagged and raw. And the seas too, now as ever gnawing and mining under the fringes of what has always seemed secure, have come rising time and again and overtaken the land, leaving behind them, when

finally they went, fossil and bed and the shape of abandoned beaches. Sea and ice and the fading power of fire have been periodic workers of this land; but always, whenever and wherever, it has been the wind and the rain, always the wind and the rain.

And so it must always have been, right from the days when the ice sheets last fell back before the gathering warmth. The winds now striking level rain into the hill behind the house can scarcely differ from those that blew here in those distant times. Is it not in this sense of continuity that lies the cause of the heart's leap and the oceanic peace felt out in the wilderness? A faint flaring of memories from out of our past, a vague awareness of ourselves as nothing but part of the wheeling processes of eternity, forever changing yet forever changeless. Close consciousness of this is perhaps long gone, for the instincts of our origins have largely been civilized out of us — yet in our response to the open land and to our mother the sea, we urbanized, computer-hounded creatures still give some acknowledgement to what was, and perhaps at heart still is, if we only knew it, at the core of all earthly existence.

The earliest settlers of this northern wilderness, one suspects, knew all and nothing of this. Dependency to the point of life or death, the greatest bond of all, must have held the Mesolithic hunter-gatherers of the sixth millennium BC so close to the earth and its beasts that it left them neither choice nor much scope for the consideration of things: their prey, and the land from which they gleaned some added sustenance, was what they were, their present and all of their future. The skeletons of two people of this misty time that were discovered in the caves near the Allt nan Uamh in Wester Ross had bones of arctic fox, reindeer, northern lynx and bear near them. Ideas that the bones were the remains of the two's food supply cross with others suggesting a simpler scene in which, over the years, the caves had merely been a place for holing up for both man and beast alike. Perhaps, though, there need be no clear distinction here: man and beast both prowling the land in pursuit of survival, making use of much the same skills and the same shelter, and from time to time eating one another, as true companions of the earth. And as berry and beast and fuel ran

6

out, so these people moved on, leaving little or no mark behind other than the occasional handful of artefacts.

Mesolithic to Neolithic to the Beaker People – the progress is immense in concept and detail, yet still but a scratching on the enormity of the wilderness land. Chambered tombs, standing stones, stone circles, dark and mysterious, speak of such spirit of intuitive understanding, of sub-mystical closeness to the earth and the star-shot sky above, that our casual way of tagging these people as 'primitive' can sometimes seem verging on the insensitive and crass. If integration is indeed the heart of happiness, what score can we be so sure of having over these silent ancestors of ours?

Letting one's mind open back to these times, it is easier to envisage the small communities with their unknown tongues and half-guessed beliefs than it is to see the now naked glens and straths packed out with woodland and wild forest. I have lain dozing doglike by a fire of peat and ancient tree-root far out in the empty grounds east of Slioch as a kiln-hot day slid on into its night; lain and dreamed waking scenes of the great forest there and another summer's night three thousand years before, with the people hunkered in the same shudder of flamelight, ever aware of the vastness of the dark, encircling wood where the bear and the boar, the wolverene and the hunting packs moved and waited. But from there to those few pale twists of branch and root thrown up from the peat by the workings of wind and rain is a stepless change all but beyond belief.

The idea of the Old Wood never quite lets go. Its shadow is always there, pressing imperceptibly at the margins of what is light and conscious in us, shaping out a memory of things, a whole way of being, that reaches beyond what, by some unconscious displacement, we now primarily concern ourselves with – the balance of nature. Measureless and numinous, full of silence and hidden sound, or surging surf-like beneath squall and gale, the primeval forest's dark impenetrability and damp chaos of undergrowth are, in one's mind's eye, a suggestion of all that we have allowed to drift away within ourselves. The shadow shape of the Old Wood is an image of the unspoken and the unspeakable, of what is in itself unclear and so seemingly dangerous. There is the possibility that our urgent and necessary concern for the balance of nature conceals another fundamental need for balance – that between ourselves and the natural world around us.

Here, where the land looks north across open sea to the islands, where the single-track road grows cockscombs of grass down its middle and where days may pass without sight of another person, there is enough of the original stillness and unpaced ways of living to give one the sensation of peering out on to an earlier world: a seeming microcosm of all that remains free and uncluttered in this country of the north. It is true, no forest can ever have grown here, I think, for the winds tear in from all sides: but it is certainly changed ground, the house adrift in a sea of lazy-beds, long giant furrows that would have given drainage to the crops and vegetables grown on the ridgebacks between. Sheep have had the grazing here for a long time now, so the ground cleared of heather and rock lies nap-soft and summer-bright, a startling warmth held between the low, knotted massings of the hills and the ocean sea. But they are nothing but bright flecks in a hard and sombre landscape, these slopes of grazing; for just beyond, along the coast at the road's end, there is only the brown and purple crush of desolation, where knuckled fists of rock crowd thrusting out into long, spined headlands, rough and cut in with pockets of quaking bog and bitter soil. It would be hard to imagine that anyone ever fought for this ground: now even the hardy sheep seem largely to hold to the grassy rims of the bays.

Being in this small, quiet corner of coast, where everything seems overwhelmed by rock and sea and enormous skies, one forms an image of life over the centuries along the country's western seaboard. Away in the lusher grounds of places like the Borders and the Black Isle, there are everywhere signs that man has succeeded in his bid to tame the land: great shaped fields smoothed and scored by ploughshare and harrow, mathematical neatness of fence and hedge and gate, farmhouse and outbuildings standing proud and strong, and always roads, big and small, roads giving swiftness to the market-place and to the bright lights of an evening's ease. The root difference here is that there is to be no such winning, nor ever has been: this is a world where the simplicity of subsistence has tended to be the level of man's ambition in his enduring struggle with the land. Those for whom this is no longer tolerable generally move away; those who stay and those, like myself, who come to seek it out, find in it a certain perspective that suits their feeling for living. It sometimes seems to me that away beyond the mountains, over on those better grounds, mankind has made its mark indelibly on the landscape; but that here in the west, and in the north, it has been the land that has made its mark on the people, the rigours and constraints of its nature shaping them to ways of calmness and acceptance.

Moons and seasons come and go and are like waymarks of assurance in the dogged passing of time. Chance and unpredictability come in among the seasons, though, cold, north-born winds with the force of storms kicking up in a trice right in the middle of summer, just as calm, open-skied days may suddenly rise out of the middle of a month of winter gales. Wind is certainly what rules here in these Atlantic parishes; and indeed seldom seems absent, especially in the half-lit time between the equinoxes. Then the old south-westerlies come pouring over the back of the hill day after day and through the nights, till the world seems nothing but a great booming place; and rain is usually with them too, in racing drifts of fine mizzling or, more often, in cataracts and flails of water that rake the walls and fill the channels of the lazy-beds till the house stands lost in a maze of sluiceways. The beginning of cabin fever can creep in when the days of storm become weeks, not least around the depths of the solstice when the night hours so far outpace the spans of light. South over the hill, where shelter gives growth to woodland, gales will tumble branch and bough against the lines and leave one unpowered and crouched by candle and oil-lamp. Lightning strike will do it too, and then even the prickling of lights in the villages far across the sea may go out. Twentieth-century man in me knows that this is a mere hiccup in technology; but the Mesolithic in me cowers in the cave, pinned down by the sheer enormity of the now and of the whole season of night, and speaks to the spirits of promise and propitiation in longing for the sight of day.

Winds from the north and north-west carry down ice streams from the Pole and rip up the sea into shreds of freezing foam that rank in against the coast. Hail rattles in with them, short frenzies of squall that process in over the sea in blocks of opaque veiling and pass on into the hills to leave the cold sunlight flaring on the whiteness and the blue. But it is the westerlies that threaten us here. They may come and blow as the other winds; but from time to time they come in the highest reaches of the Beaufort scale as true destroyers. Then it is a time for securing and for taking up the slack on rope and hawser, of watching and waiting and holding on to faith. Below the headland, sea changes happen then: a pure evilness of mud colouring coming into the water so that the great rollers passing along the coast are of putrid and cream messing. The rock shore itself is half-gone, surf and air no longer separate, and the burst of waves is sucked and driven up a hundred foot of cliff into grape-shot and hurricane mist. The back of ridges, well down, enclose vacuum holes of peace; but ten paces higher, as one comes up for the crossing, crazings of windstream and turbulence may have you knocked down, tangled and plucked about.

Perhaps just because it is such a place of winds, much of the joy in a life here has to do with the sudden moments of calm. A day thick with sea-mist and hanging stillness and the long, regular breathing of the fog-horn far away at the point can bring such intensity, such an awareness of everything, from the silent passing of a gull in the mist to the measured strike of one's own heart. Or a day of showers and slow movement of clouds out over the islands, with the gleam of sun there and gone on the sea through the hours; and the evening following in full of the rare warmth of contentment. And then another day's

end going out in similar quiet but an awakening from a dream in the small hours showing a light swell shooting up pale, drum-beat plumes of spray off the rocks under a clear, full moon. And those sunlit days of winter when the snow lies firm and only the laziest of winds curls over the ground; and, with the sheep away down for the grass, the world seeming suddenly quite empty and clean and new. But perhaps beyond all are the days of spring and early summer, with the long winter past and the wonder of all earthly renewal filling one, body and soul. Days on end often quite without rain, hot and calm, and the sun falling away out to sea so late that there is light for walking the hill past midnight:

> . . . *coolness and deathless pearl*
> *Of afterlight above, a canopy*
> *Bursting with lambs crying out*
> *And away, deep by the wood*
> *Of the coiling burn,*
> *Cuckoo, midnight cuckoo,*
> *Calling everlasting, such sheerness of season.*

On the whole we see only handfuls of visitors out this way. Unless they are walkers or geologists, there is in any case little for them to do other than to drive to the end of the road and turn round; or make the short excursion down to the cave where St Columba reputedly baptized some sixth-century footpads (one senses that the holy man's schedule must have been on the tight side with all the things he is said to have done). Talk still goes on, as it has for twenty years, about blasting an extension of the road on over the hills to link up with the tourist routes out from the town. It is the old story, of the appeal of convenience and profit, today's bywords, set against the beauty that is inextricably part of the quiet of remoteness.

So much part of the wilderness land are the creatures of its open and hidden spaces. Symbol and essence of everything that stands outside and separate from the workings of man, their attunement to the ground of their habitat can make one feel all but out of place, a misfit, as one goes stalking by. Deer are everywhere about, blended in and still, yet there if one waits. The long days of summer find them high up; but earlier in the year, when feeding is poor and sleet makes a raw misery of the hill, they will be down in search of anything that is half-succulent and green. In the warmth of June, their wing-eared calves lie coiled under peat hag and bank, all knobble knee and glossy eye. But with the year passing over into autumn, there is a memory I have of walking the snowy hill by moonlight, with deep frost and the flitter of a honed wind; and the luminous night filled with the rage and defiance of two stags in the rut, enlarged and redoubled by the mountain echo. And then again, far from the snows of that night, a moment of dreamlike mystery on a headland of the sea in haze and leaden sunlight, seeing the antlered shape of a stag offshore as it swam out for the grazing of an island.

The wildcat, fox, pine marten and otter are here too. The cat, nocturnal and reclusive, is more often than not just a large, ringed tail vanishing from the car's headlights; but not long back, one came trotting by after breakfast, a small tiger, and with two kits prancing along behind. A vent in the limestone close to the house is also a cat place, a store for dead gulls – but maybe nothing is quite that cut and dried in the natural world, for twice recently I have met an otter, dark and serpentine, lolloping up the hill to the same den. And now the gulls have gone.

But in the airiness and elation of this world above the ocean, it is perhaps the hunting birds, all grace and impetuous intent, that seem to be the spirit incarnate of wilderness living. Eagles, by their span and absolute power of the columns of air, are to me mostly birds of distance and majesty. One, surprised high in the hills, merely looked up at me from its feeding and then lazily opened its wings on to the gale, to become in a blink a mote beneath the clouds. Sea eagles too pass by along the coast from time to time, birds almost ponderous in their size. In fact, it is to the smaller, lither hunters that the eye springs, hunters that come and are gone all in the same moment; for they are the ones that make mockeries of gravity and play with the air, the ones whose speeding and precision in the chase seem to the human eye all effortless joy. Sparrowhawks, attackers by surprise, come out of the birch wood that grows up the burn, and hunt low and fast, hurdling walls, pulling tight round boulders, ever alert for the rise of startled wings. I saw a thrush, panic-spurred, slip over a bluff; the hawk, at full stretch and a yard from the rock, braked up on open wings and tail into a backward somersault and came perfectly to rest on a stone. At other times, leaving off from this dauntlessness, they will fly high and wingspread, soaring against the sun on warmth and current, quite another bird. Once, deep in a low, silent wood, I came on the remains of one lying askew amid a mess of its own fluff and feather at the foot of some other bird's plucking-post – the large owl, perhaps, that had passed by mothlike and soundless as I walked higher in the wood a dusk or two earlier.

Falcons, all pectoral and scythe of wing, fling themselves across the great open skies. The little kestrel swings and slides on the wind, taking up his stances, watching eye-still out of his shimmering hold on the air, dropping, peeling away, day after day. Even smaller, the merlin comes as a dim streak at the edge of one's vision, fleet over the ground and away; or a bullet shape, swift and swerving, escaping over one's head down a wooded ravine. But the peregrine, which wanders high in the heavens, hidden by distance and light for the hunt, is the bird of utter fearlessness, of miracle speed and poise. Peregrine

and gull once passed feet from my window in level pursuit; another, announced by the alarm cries of geese in the next bay, floated dark and menacing over the ridge to burst among a cloud of starlings and shepherd one apart. On a day of breeze and sunshine, I watched one through the glasses as she rose, steady in beat and glide, out above the hills and upwards strongly into a clear sky. On and on she went, mounting the air, till her form was so deep in the blue that drunkenness began to fill my head. At last, up on the outer edges, she opened into broad turns, once, twice, and then on an instant heeled sharply over and dropped out of the sky. Wings drawn in, she was a stone falling, a plummeting gathering for some impossible attack:

> There where the falcon strikes,
> There whither she is drawn
> Down from her peripheries of blue
> In steepening arcs,
> Bounding in falls of fearless joy,
> That rupture the decorous,
> Hew through the chasteness,
> Invade the unmapped, the long shifting voids,
> As she comes, streaming in madness and perfecting grace,
> In pursuit of all she knows yet knows not why . . .

She fell the full length of the summer sky and, still falling, vanished behind the hills.

From headland to headland, in cliff and chaos of rock and a scattering of bays, this line of coast runs ten miles and holds just that many households. With the expanse of the land and the greater stretches of the sea, it is hard not to see man as somehow incidental here. A tractor toils slowly up a slope; a single boat stands off the coast working the trawl backwards and forwards; a man, bent leaning on his crook out on the ridge above the sea, calls and whistles his dogs to the gathering of the sheep. But later, a minute or an hour, they are gone and the passing of the day is once more measured by a shower, a change of wind, a rainbow suddenly rooted in the open sea.

Yet it is also a time of changes. Inland from here, the hill was put under the forestry plough some years ago and now sports the deep, harsh scorings with their ranks of conifer. Like most plantations, it is a closed-off, dead sort of place to walk through, even on the brightest of days, the files of trees quite without the spirit feeling that is part of the smallest wood of nature. Further over still, on the south side, the loch lies glutted with the fish-farms, moorings of steel cages where the finless salmon hordes crowd to receive their antibiotics and antibacterials and colouring agents before being hauled away south by the ton in the big lorries. On this side, the fisherman sets his bag nets in the ancient manner for the run of wild fish, clean and muscle-firm from the ocean journey, and must settle for what chance and the seals will allow him . . . The little hut of a post-office is reduced to part-time; back over the hill, the hotel, catching somebody's eye, is bought up and inflated by refurbishment and luxury. Out at the point, at this world's end, the lighthouse is to be unmanned: the watchful and the human no more, the squat tower now a dozing automaton. This would certainly seem to be the way of things these days. Development and the drive for efficiency being forced in side by side with a dogged holding to all that is age-old and paced slow by the seasons. Jobs and styles of living may shift and change but this even pacing of the days will always remain the substance of an ease of heart.

Moments of some sudden chthonic force seem to remain like a branding. There was an all but darkless night of midsummer spent encamped on a peak high above the coast, when I lay sleepless, seeing myself held in floating equilibrium between the thousands of feet of rock pressing up into my back and the greater thousands of giddying air weighing lightly upon me from above. Or another night, here, with a swollen ascendant moon out over the sea, and the fields of the sky clustered thick with star and milkiness, and the sound only of soft surf at the headland coming on the steadiness of a warm breeze. And a sudden insistence of feeling that the house, my home, was really by the by, that it was only the land, the moonlit land before me that was important . . . But before this, one winter's day long ago in Coigach, I left the road and walked over a low pass to climb a mountain. The day was full of high winds from the north, bringing down rhythms of snow across a sharp blue sky. Snow lay over the last two thousand feet of the climb but I found a gully route and went straight for the top, tucking down for moments when the barrages of storms came in. I rose out of the gully as a squall passed away south and headed up the long frozen slope to the cairn whose tip peeped out of the deep snow. There at the top, everything was crackle-frosted and swept by a shining wind: on all sides, the snow-backs and glintering lochans, while far away west the long shape of Lewis lying low on the sea. The sky was clear; the next storm still some way off to the north. Then, as I stood there, an enormous shadow passed swiftly over me. Twisting round, I fell back into the snow and lay there, quite unable to move, for several minutes, staring through wind-watering eyes up at the brilliance of the empty sky.

The dull, ringing strike of the axe deep in the forest still resounds within mind and forgotten memory. Stone and flint, then bronze and iron and steel, the axe-heads flashing in the sunlight had begun to eat away at the edges of what was obscure and threatening. With this, the end of our passivity had come: now we would seek to impose our will on things and to shape nature to our needs. So dark forest, and all its spirit awe, dwindled; and out in the newly created open, the building began. Modern, civilized man had been born.

But the education and enlightenment that eventually became the mark of modern man were inevitably to be things that flourished in the places of building and people. By simple weight of size and market power, towns were soon the centre of all learning as well; and so the countryside and its folk fell progressively into disrepute, as regions of old superstition and backwardness. There, far from the shadowless light of science and academic knowledge, the spirit of the Old Wood lingered on – as it always will anywhere that has not been entombed in concrete and cement. But even now, in both town and country, one still senses its presence most strongly in the minds of young children, as yet intact, with their closeness to all feeling, with their wonder and fantasy and fear mixing so easily with reason and what we like to call reality. The learning of education and all the attitudes of the adult world soon put a stop to that though, when emphasis is placed on fact and figure, and scorn of the mysterious and the unknowable is only lightly veiled.

This scorn, I think, and the arrogance that goes with it, is inherent in the very concept of towns. For order, structure, reason and fact are the essence of the creation of these conglomerations. Towns are the places for all that is merely clever and ingeniously brilliant in man, for technical expertise and the machineries of management; the places that prove by demonstration our total control over nature, our ability to suppress anything that is wayward or unruly. Verticals and right-angles and the eternal neatness of symmetry hold sway; circles and ellipses are to perfection, even curves are regular and smooth. Towns are a celebration, a monument to what we can achieve by skill.

But they are also a memorial to the quiet, inner death suffered by those living in them. For in making these great sprawls of places, which involves the closing out, the burying of nature, we stand to close out and destroy some part of ourselves. Born as creatures of the earth, we have a need to feel ourselves within and part of the great patterns of the natural world; without this earth-rooting, we are open to a gradual process of fragmentation and loss. Maybe it is through some vague dismay about this that we make areas of our towns into parks and gardens, in an effort to bring something of nature back again and so alleviate the suffocation of urban days. But a scattering of flowers, a few level squares of lawn and some trees with iron guards are a sad likeness of the countryside and one that gives no ease or joy. And with the flowers, there is the constant traffic growl, the smutted haze, the tarmac and the tower blocks, the sirens, the flight path and all the desolation that is a city park.

But let the towns be. Maybe generations of their smoke and

speed and noise have indeed evolved some kind of separate sub-species that thrives on such things and for whom the prospect of country living would only suggest a death by boredom. Certainly, there is nothing to do here, in a city sense, nor any kind of busyness to keep one forgetful of oneself; whereas towns can provide some of the antidotes for feelings of tedium and jadedness. Towns were my origins, yet ever since coming to this part of the world, there has been a strong sense of coming back. And in these years of being settled here, I have found myself with another sense of rightness, a closeness – not to the people of the immediate past nor even to the brave souls who worked these lazy-beds and who were so shamefully evicted back in 1853. Nor for that matter to any of the people of historical times. There is something else in me though, something residing quite easily within the twentieth-century framework of my mind, that is full of a closeness to those peoples of our prehistory. I harbour no secret hankerings for a life in a cave, or even a diet of berries and half-raw flesh; nor in fact do I have any Rousseauesque illusions about the noble savage. Yet the spirit of those times and of the people that inhabited them is very much part of my daily living. Often, both by twilight and under the stillness of a hot sun, they are suddenly closer than ever: I round rocks expecting to find a group of them there, looking up at me from over a kill; unconsciously I lean my ear to the wind in the hope of catching the distant thunk of a stone axe at work. Out on the hill, I stop in my tracks and stare up at a deer on the opposite slope and feel that sudden and violent bond of sureness and veneration, of distance and closeness, of a linking of creatures, of the Mesolithic hunter catching sight of a way to his future in front of him. For an instant, the immediacy of food, and of coupling later in the cave, and the two together making up faith of hope, are all one again. I shake my head but for another few moments yet the whole business of culture and civilization seems remote and anodyne.

I think this is simply a visual and mental imaging of how I believe the land seemed to people when they were still truly part of it, in the way that the beasts still are today. Once there were huts and houses, men and women had already become one stage removed and the land was outside and merely there for their use. From this point through to the chequered monotony of the landscape of modern commercial farming is one long haul of technical progress and spiritual diffusion.

The fading of spiritual identity is the sadness of modern times – spirit, that is, not in any church (let alone denominational) sense but in the context of our holding a strong image of ourselves in proportion to the eternal. The outward expression of this inner vision might be said to be a sense of wonder, a living awareness of the inexplicable yet strangely purposeful natural world around us. These patterns and paradoxes in nature are the elements to which the early peoples gave the names of gods; and gods with human characteristics like anger and spite and jealousy, who were present in nature and, as it were, very much part of the human community. But when monotheistic Christianity arrived with its remote and ultimately absent deity and urged people away from such earthiness towards some kind of transcendence of spirit (the word now suddenly imbued with new metaphysical connotations) and otherworldliness, our roots in the soil were irrevocably wrenched loose.

Science, and the precision of knowledge, that has been the religion of this century would seem to have ensured that those roots have now been burned off for good. Yet this same masterful science has gone no way to satisfying the other questing that has always been in us; nor, I imagine, would it accept the postulation that the truth of things can only lie in the simultaneous acceptance of opposites – the known and the unknowable, just as light and dark, positive and negative, male and female: the integration and the whole. Wonder as the expression of joy in the unknowable, running side by side with our ever-increasing knowledge of the knowable; a pathway through both open sunlight and the Old Wood at the same time. Is this no more than a dream?

Swordle Chorrach, Ardnamurchan, April 1989

PART ONE   THE LUMINOUS WIND

...a curlew cried and in the luminous wind
A curlew answered;

W. B. YEATS, 'PAUDEEN'

The Lairig Ghru, Cairngorm Mountains, from the south, 1988

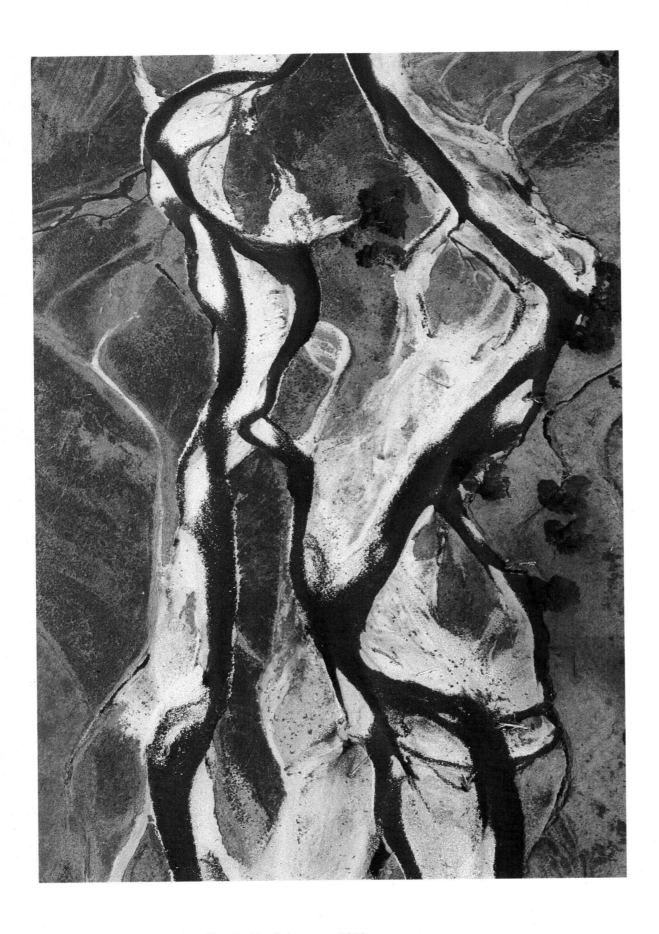

Braided river and ancient pines, Glen Feshie, Cairngorms, 1988

Lochan Uaine (The Green Lochan) below the Angel's Peak of Carn an t-Sabhail, Cairngorms, 1988

Summits of the Cairngorm plateau from above Braeriach, 1985

The Lairig Ghru, Cairngorms, 1988

Screees and valley floor sediments, Glen Derry, Cairngorms, 1985

Loch Etchachan and Loch A'an, Cairngorms, 1988

Overleaf: Solifluction lobes (patterns made by the movement of soil downhill), Lurcher's Gully, Cairngorms, 1988

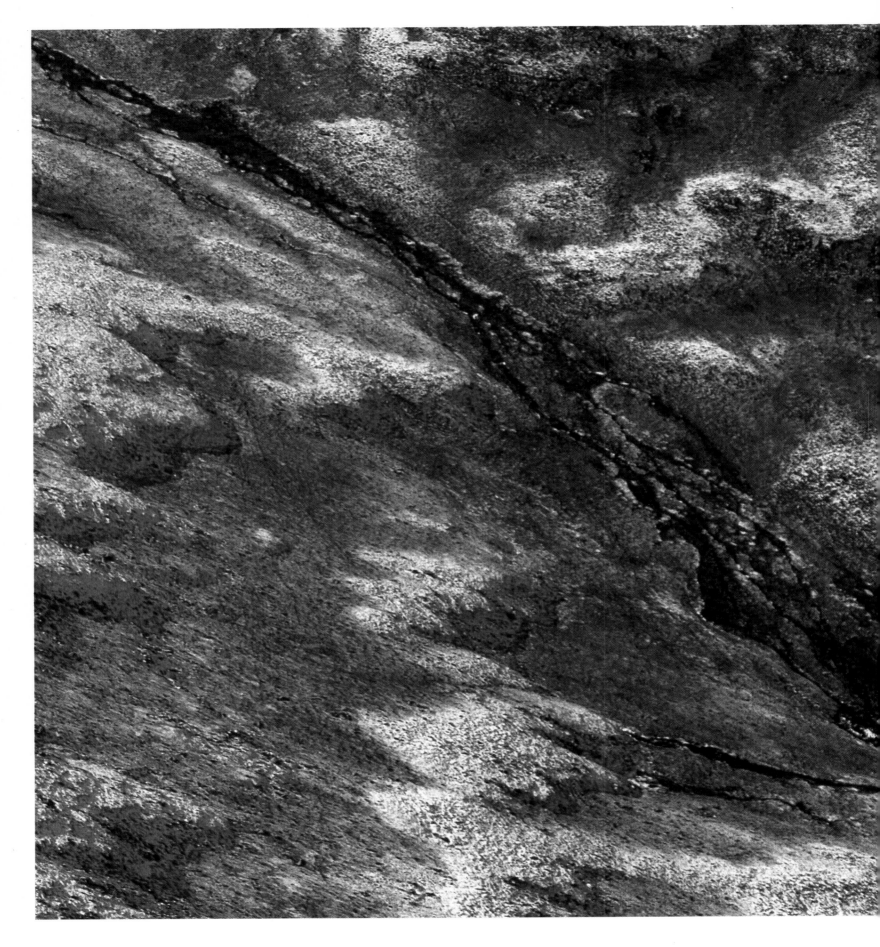

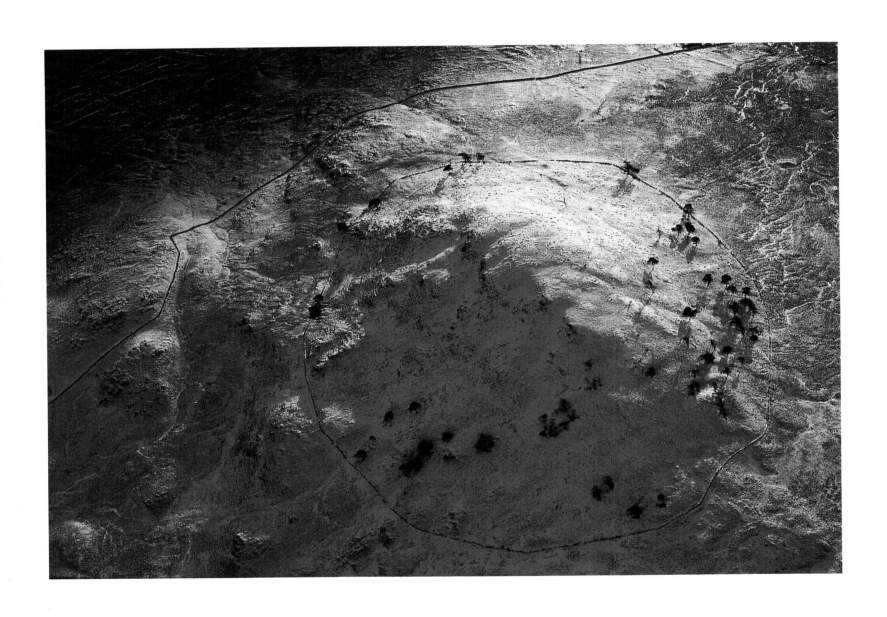

Enclosed hillock, Ben Lawers, Tayside, 1985

Caledonian pine forest and young spruce plantation, Glen Lui, Cairngorms, 1988

PART TWO   HONEY AND SALT

Honey and salt – land smell and sea smell,
as in the long ago, as in forever.

The days pick me up and carry me off,
half-child, half-prisoner,

on their journey that I'll share
for a while.

They wound and they bless me
with strange gifts:

the salt of absence,
the honey of memory.

NORMAN MACCAIG, 'BETWEEN MOUNTAIN AND SEA'

Crofts and ancient rocks, Manish, East Harris, Outer Hebrides, 1986

Castle Island and cracking ice, Loch Leven, 1987

Peat cuttings and shielings on the 'String Road', Lewis, Outer Hebrides, 1986

Crofts, Loch Eport, North Uist, Outer Hebrides, 1986

Nineteenth-century crofting patterns, Ness, Lewis, Outer Hebrides, 1986

Tantallon Castle and cliffs, East Lothian, 1985

Crofts, Geary, Vaternish, Isle of Skye, 1986

Croft house, Lewis, Outer Hebrides, 1986

Woods and Kilchurn Castle, Loch Awe, 1986

PART THREE   THE 'GOLDEN EMBLEM'

The salmon come from the sea. Men
go out on it. The *Valhalla*, the *Golden Emblem*
come in, smoking with gulls,
from the fishing grounds of the Minch.

NORMAN MACCAIG, 'A MAN IN ASSYNT'

Harbour, St Abbs, Berwickshire, 1988

Stake nets set for salmon, Lunan Bay, Angus, 1988

Salmon nets, Ethie Haven, Angus, 1988

The Eildon Hills and the River Tweed from Bemersyde, Borders, 1987

Farmhouse and steading, East Lothian, 1986

Overleaf: Fields and Traprain Law, East Lothian, 1986

Stromness, Orkney Islands, after the departure of the ferry, 1986

Heather-burning patterns, Lammermuir Hills, 1988

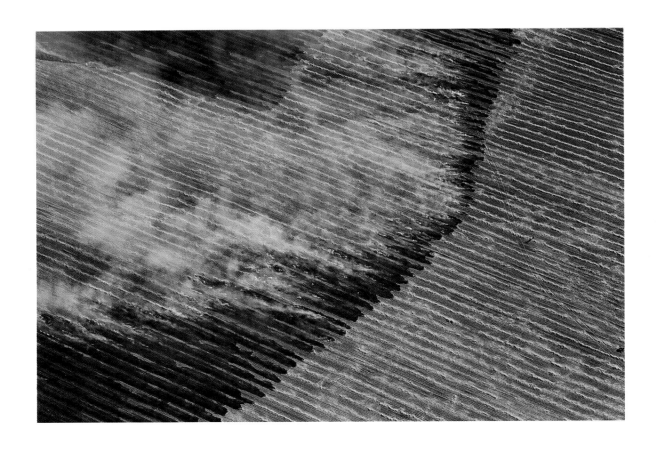

Stubble-burning, East Lothian, 1988

Stubble-burning near Montrose, Angus, 1988

PART FOUR   CAVES OF GUILT ... PINNACLES OF JUBILATION

City of everywhere, broken necklace in the sun,
you are caves of guilt, you are pinnacles of jubilation.

NORMAN MACCAIG, 'DROP-OUT IN EDINBURGH'

Edinburgh: the Castle, the medieval Old Town and the Georgian New Town, 1982

Rainbow at Silverknowes, Edinburgh, 1987

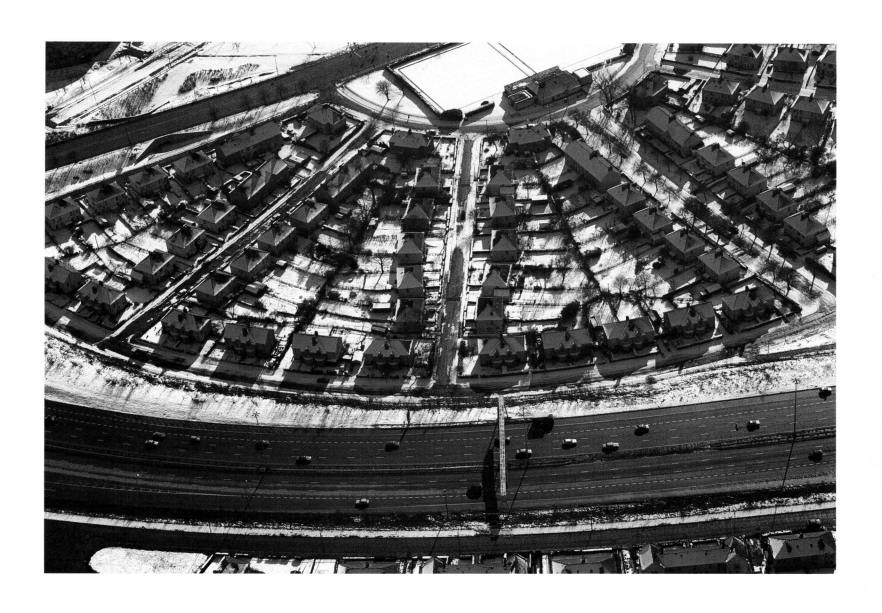

The Kennyhill and Riddrie Housing Scheme, Glasgow, 1986

Children's playground, Guy Fawkes bonfire ready to be lit, and council housing, Craigmillar, Edinburgh, 4 November 1988

Colinton Mains Park in the snow, Edinburgh, 1986

The National Gallery of Scotland, Waverley Station and part of Princes Street Gardens, Edinburgh, winter 1986

PART FIVE   A HEAVEN ON EARTH

Beneath him, with new wonder, now he views,
To all delight of human sense exposed,
In narrow room Nature's whole wealth; yea, more! –
A Heaven on Earth: for blissful Paradise
Of God the garden was, by Him in the east
Of Eden planted.

JOHN MILTON, **PARADISE LOST**

Ornamental lake and boathouse, Gosford, East Lothian, 1988

Tree nursery and woodland, Dalkeith, Midlothian, 1988

Mausoleum and trees, Gosford, East Lothian, 1988

London Road and Royal Terrace, Edinburgh, with trees, winter 1986

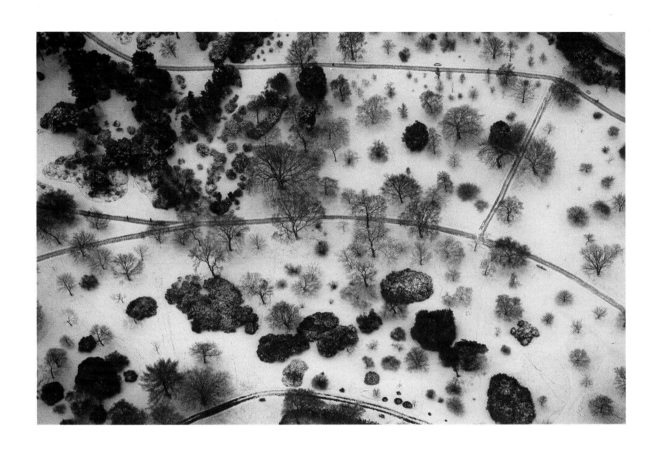

Arboretum under snow, Royal Botanic Garden, Edinburgh, 1986

Tree-felling and ruins of Old Parish Church, Tyninghame House, East Lothian, 1988

Felled grove, Tyninghame House, East Lothian, 1988

Drummond Castle and formal gardens, Tayside, 1985

62

St Michael's House and St Michael's Church, Inveresk, with Brunton's Wireworks, Musselburgh, behind, Midlothian, 1988

PART SIX   AND THE MACHINES SAY...

And the machines say, laughing
up what would have been sleeves
in the old days: 'We are at
your service.' 'Take us', we cry,

'to the places that are far off
from yourselves.' And so they do
at a price that is the alloy in
the thought that we can do without them.

R. S. THOMAS, 'FUEL'

Road, Loch Finsbay, East Harris, Outer Hebrides, 1986

Lighthouse, the Bass Rock, East Lothian, 1987

The 'West Highland' railway line crossing the Moor of Rannoch, 1986

New Lanark village and mills, with the Falls of Clyde, Lanark, 1986

'Superquarry', Glensanda, from the island of Lismore, Loch Linnhe, 1987

Coast road and windswept woods, Gosford, East Lothian, 1986

Motorway on embankment, West Lothian, 1986

Segregated traffic/pedestrian system, Cumbernauld New Town, 1986

Grangemouth Docks and Longannet Power Station on the River Forth, 1986

PART SEVEN   THE FURROW DRAWN BY ADAM'S FINGER

O Merlin in your crystal cave
Deep in the diamond of the day,
Will there ever be a singer
Whose music will smoothe away
The furrow drawn by Adam's finger
Across the meadow and the wave?

EDWIN MUIR, 'MERLIN'

Partly ploughed field, Strathclyde, 1986

Oilseed rape field, East Lothian, 1985

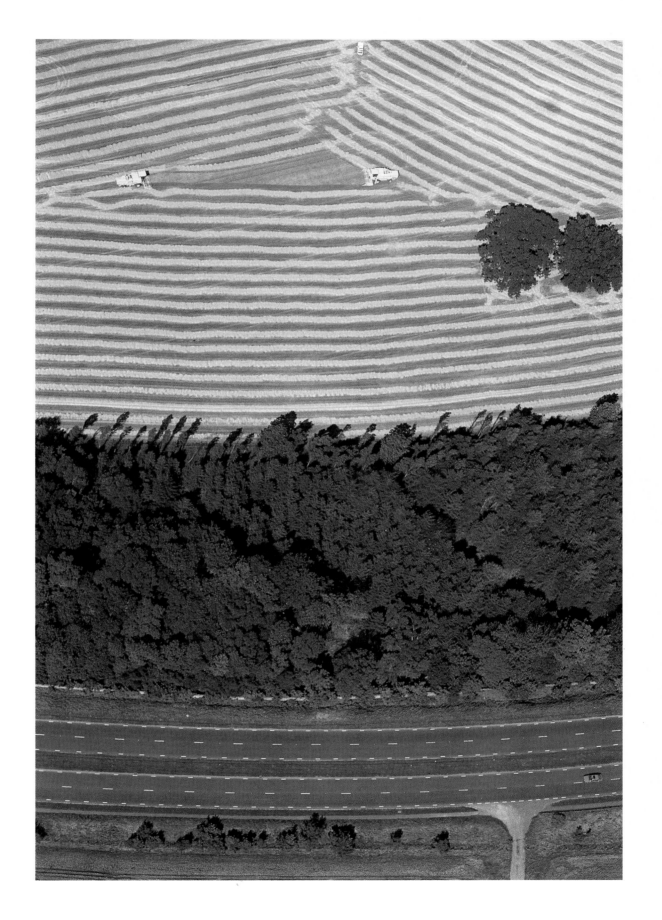

Combine harvesters, the Carse of Gowrie, 1988

Rape fields, Fife, 1987

The shed

Overleaf: Heather moor with Scots pines, and plantation of spruce firs, Tayside, 1987

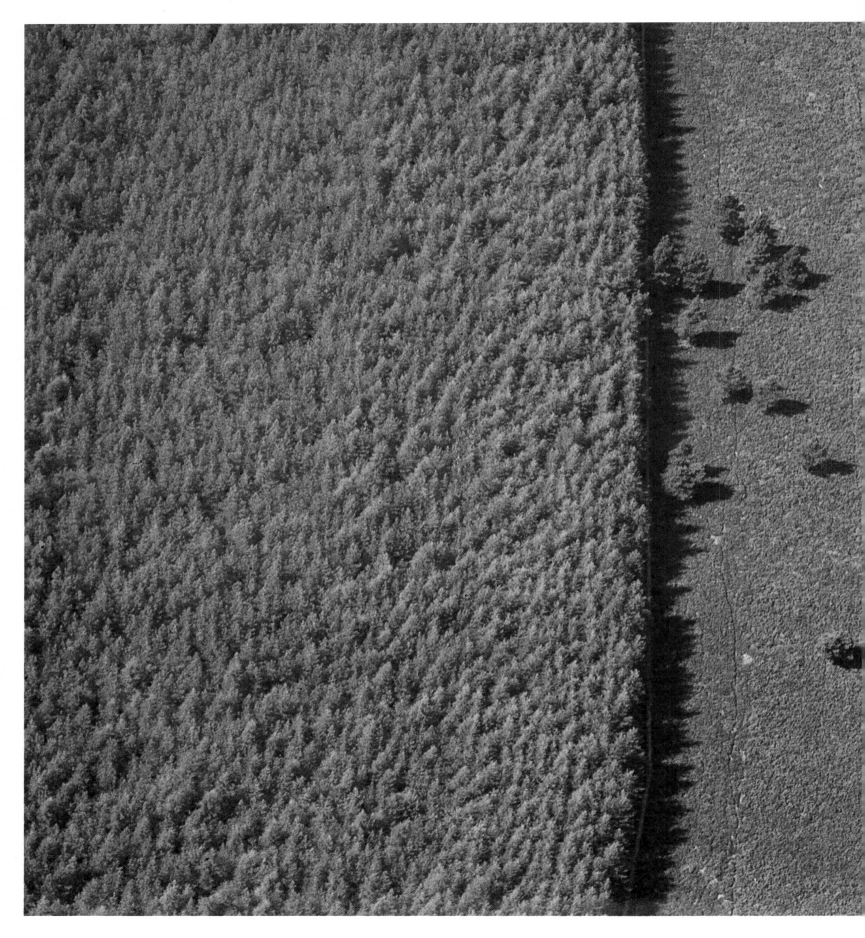

Spraying fertilizer on forest, Galloway, 1986

Patterned mire and dying forest, the Flow Country, Caithness, 1988

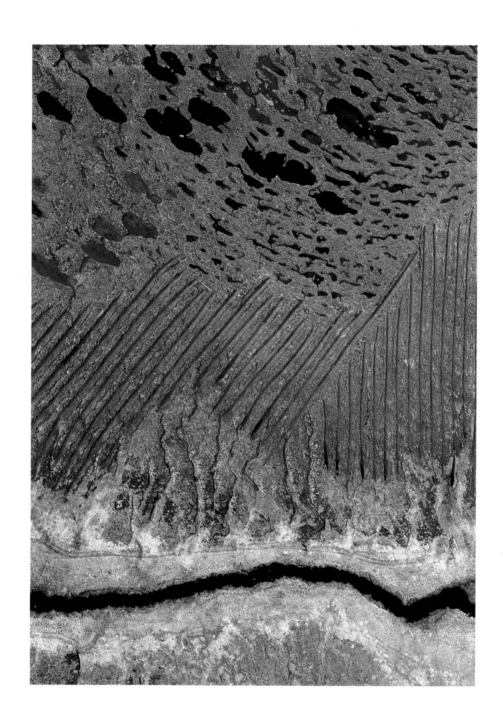

Patterned mire and forestry drainage ditches, the Flow Country, Caithness, 1988

Blanket bog and felled forest, the Great Glen, 1987

PART EIGHT   THESE DARKENED FIELDS

But famished field and blackened tree
Bear flowers in Eden never known.
Blossoms of grief and charity
Bloom in these darkened fields alone.
What had Eden ever to say
Of hope and faith and pity and love
Until was buried all its day
And memory found its treasure trove?
Strange blessings never in Paradise
Fall from these beclouded skies.

EDWIN MUIR, 'ONE FOOT IN EDEN'

Wanlockhead village and abandoned lead mines, Leadhills, Southern Uplands, 1986

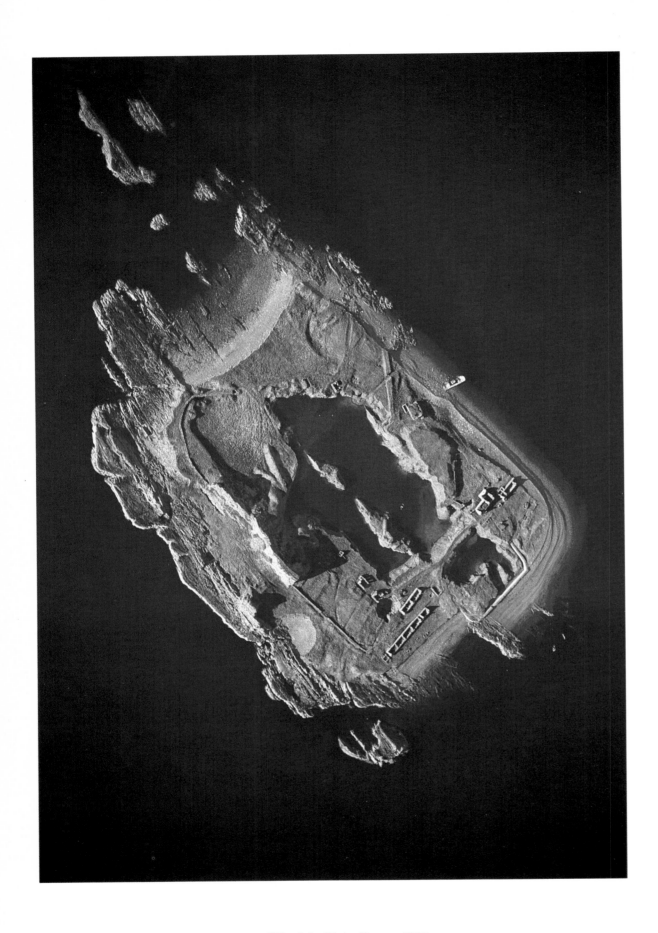

Belnahua Island and flooded slate quarries, off Easdale, Firth of Lorne, 1988

Smoking coal bing and housing estate, West Lothian, 1986

Ruins of colliery and saltworks, Preston Island, and land reclamation lagoons of Longannet Power Station, Fife, 1986

Housing, Easterhouse, Glasgow, 1986

Shipyards, Clydebank, Glasgow, 1986

Second World War block ship, Hoy Sound, Orkney Islands, 1986

Oil slick from wreck of HMS *Royal Oak*, sunk during the Second World War, Scapa Flow, Orkney Islands, 1986

Iron Age hillfort and Torness Power Station, East Lothian, 1989

PART NINE   MAN-INFECTED, MAN-PROTECTED

Leisure hills, motorway connected.
Fashioned ski-ing hills, quality inspected.
Hills with plastic huts erected.
Hills where economic gain's detected.
Hills the planning men corrected.
Hills injected, hills dissected.
Hills the TV resurrected;
man-infected, man-protected.

ROBIN MUNRO, 'HILLS'

Ski-tows, Coire Cas, Cairngorms, 1988

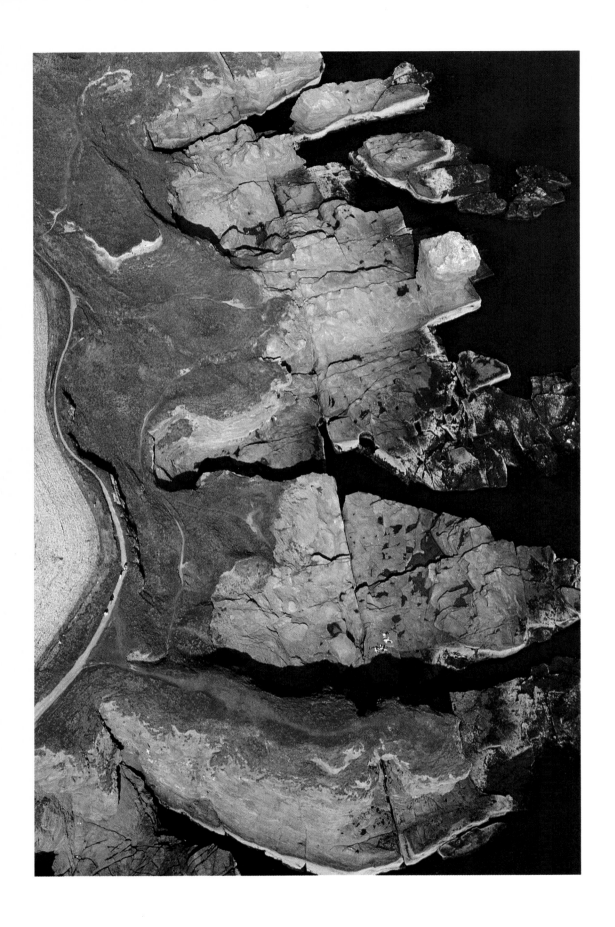

Day out by the Deil's Heid rock near Arbroath, Angus, 1988

Riding on the shore, Belhaven, East Lothian, 1986

Boat in garden, Pittenweem, Fife, 1988

Scottish Mining Museum (Lady Victoria Colliery) and miners' 'rows', Newtongrange, Midlothian, 1986

Yacht marina, Inverkip, Clyde estuary, 1986

Scottish Exhibition Centre and Glasgow Garden Festival on the River Clyde, Glasgow, 1988

'Savacentre'and sports facilities, Edinburgh, 1988

Petrochemical complex, motorway and golf course, Grangemouth, Central, 1986

PART TEN EARTH WAS THE ONLY MEETING PLACE

The angel and the girl are met.
Earth was the only meeting place.
For the embodied never yet
Travelled beyond the shore of space.
The eternal spirits in freedom go.

See, they have come together, see,
While the destroying minutes flow,
Each reflects the other's face
Till heaven in hers and earth in his
Shine steady there. He's come to her
From far beyond the farthest star,
Feathered through time. Immediacy
Of strangest strangeness is the bliss
That from their limbs all movement takes.
Yet the increasing rapture brings
So great a wonder that it makes
Each feather tremble on his wings.

Outside the window footsteps fall
Into the ordinary day
And with the sun along the wall
Pursue their unreturning way.
Sound's perpetual roundabout
Rolls its numbered octaves out
And hoarsely grinds its battered tune.

But through the endless afternoon
These neither speak nor movement make,
But stare into their deepening trance
As if their gaze would never break.

EDWIN MUIR, 'THE ANNUNCIATION'

Tents by the rocks, Carlingheugh Bay, Angus, 1988

Symbols, Calton Hill, Edinburgh, 1987

Integrated farming and forestry near Selkirk, Borders, 1986

Overleaf: Canoeists approach the sea, East Lothian, 1986

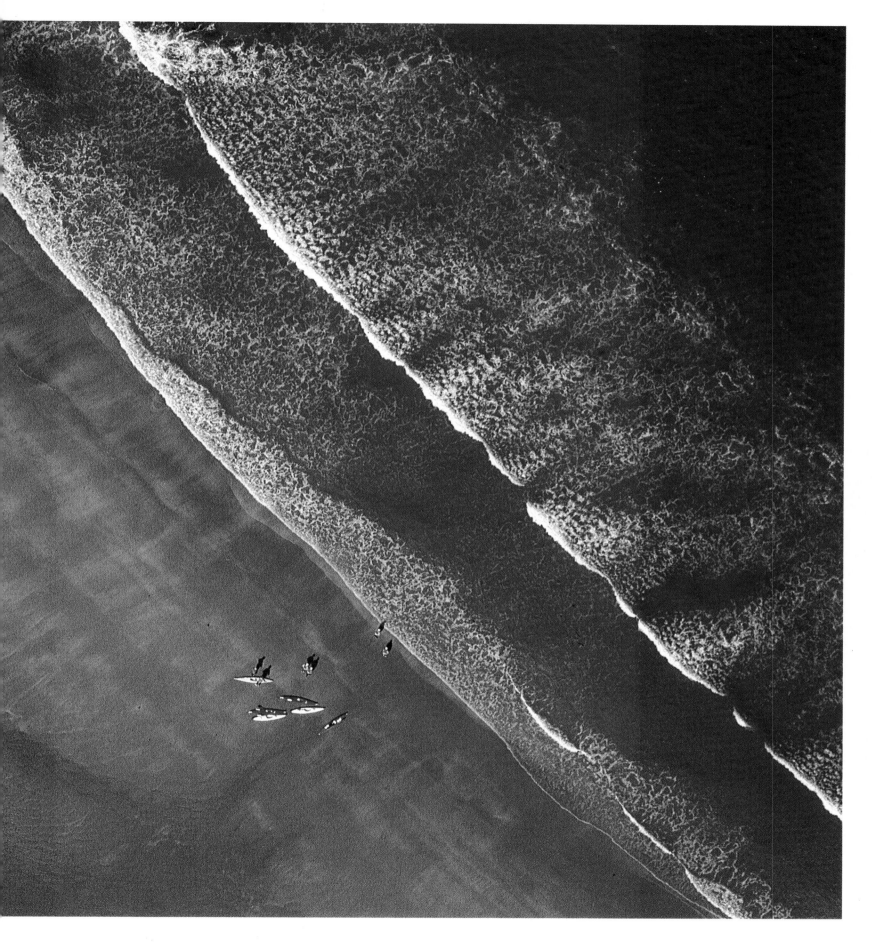

NOTES ON THE PHOTOGRAPHS

PART ONE
THE LUMINOUS WIND

*Did the sun grow the tree that made the
paper you are holding, and the ink on it, so
that it can read this book through your eyes?
    The eye as a kind of scanner for the sun
is an idea with a glimpse of God in it. It is
knowledge.*

Guy Davenport, *The Geography of the
Imagination*

The Cairngorm Mountains are by far the largest
mass of really high 'arctic' land in the British
Isles. Although they cannot truly be described
as 'wilderness' in the strict sense, the landscape
here, shown on pp. 13-21 and 23, is probably
the most natural that still exists in Britain today.
The glaciated mountain scenery has many fine
features and, although the land may appear to
be inhospitable to living creatures, the plant
and animal life is rich, especially in montane
or northern species. The presence of the
surrounding woods (which represent part of a
once-continuous tract of forest land – the 'Old
Caledonian Forest' – although they are today
semi-natural rather than natural) is a significant
aspect of the outstanding nature conservation
interest in the Cairngorm area.

    Various developments are taking place in
and around the Cairngorms, most notably the
expansion of skiing activity (see p. 97) and
tourism. The northern slopes of the mountain
massif are particularly affected. There is an
active debate about the future of the area, in
particular about appropriate forms of statutory
conservation protection, and a great deal
of public concern and involvement with
'wilderness' areas has become focused on
the Cairngorm issue. Concern for mountain
landscapes is particularly intense in Scots the
world over. The feeling may be summed up in
the words of John Muir, an early international
pioneer of the modern environment movement,
born in Dunbar in East Lothian: 'Going to the
mountains is going home.'

    The Lairig Ghru, shown on pp. 13 and 17,
is a particularly dramatic glaciated valley which
runs approximately north-west to south-east
through the Cairngorms between some of the
highest peaks, Braigh Riabhach (Braeriach)
and Carn an t-Sabhail (Cairn Toul) to the west
and Beinn MacDuibh (Ben Macdui) and Cairn
Lochan to the east. It is a popular walkers'
route. The photograph on p. 13 shows the Lairig
from the south, with shadow on the Devil's
Point, the lower conical hill on the left, and
sunlight on the higher sharp peak behind it, the
Angel's Peak of Carn an t-Sabhail. The semi-
natural pine forest surrounding the main
mountain massif is shown on the left of the
photograph on p. 23. The heather moor and
open woodland vegetation of large old Scots
pines is threatened here in Glen Lui by forestry
plantations of spruce like the one shown at the
right.

PART TWO
HONEY AND SALT

*The imagination has a history, as yet
unwritten, and it has a geography, as yet
only dimly seen. History and geography
are inextricable disciplines.*

Guy Davenport, *The Geography of the
Imagination*

The life of the croft and that of the castle are two
principal features of the romantic view of
Scottish history. While some of the romance
was, and is, undoubtedly founded on fact, the
harsher realities, as well as the true humanity
sometimes also obscured by the romance, of
many of the lives lived in these landscapes
should not be forgotten.

    Page 26 shows an island stronghold which
was one of the prisons, in the sixteenth century,
of the unfortunate Mary, Queen of Scots. Mary
escaped, in highly romantic fashion, from this
castle in 1568 with the help of George and
Willie Douglas, the brother and young cousin of
Sir William Douglas, the master of the castle,
both of whom had become and remained
devoted to her. She very soon lost her freedom
once more, however, following the defeat of her
troops at the battle of Langside, near Glasgow,
after which she fled to England, only to be
incarcerated in a succession of English castles
until her eventual beheading on the orders of
her cousin, Queen Elizabeth I of England, in
1587. Willie Douglas remained with her until
her death. The unusual ice patterns on the
frozen surface of the loch resulted from a long
spell of very cold weather; such patterns are
usually found only in polar regions.

    Tantallon Castle, shown on page 30, was
built in the fourteenth century, one of the last
of the large baronial courtyard castles of the
medieval period. It had a justified reputation for
impregnability, giving rise to the local saying
'as soon ding doon Tantallon', referring to
some impossible task. Its powerful owners
successfully resisted sieges by the monarch of
the day on two occasions, and the castle was
overcome only with great difficulty by the forces
of Oliver Cromwell in 1650, at a time when this
type of military architecture had long been
rendered obsolete by the development of
artillery, and by changing economic and
political conditions.

    As other photographs in this part (on pp.
25, 27, 28, 29, 31 and 32) show, crofting,
although an ancient way of life, is still a living
reality in Scotland, particularly in the western
Highlands and Islands. There are today
probably around 10,000 people who make up
the crofting community. The position of the
crofter in the present day could not be better
described than has been done by James Hunter
in his excellent and comprehensive book, *The
Making of the Crofting Community*:

*Numerically insignificant and
geographically distant from the centres of
British industry, trade and political power,
crofters exercise no great influence on the
country as a whole. Nor have they done so in
the past. Crofters and their families are,
however, a distinctive social group. They
possess their own culture, speak their own*

language and generally live their lives in a way long since abandoned in the rest of Britain. The uniqueness of the crofting way of life – itself a reason for studying the crofting past – has long been apparent. At one time it tended to provoke in outsiders a desire to sweep crofters and crofting into the dustbin of history and to remake the Highlands in the image of the southern British countryside. Today, principally because of the steady erosion of the nineteenth-century belief in the self-evident virtue of 'progress', a quite opposite reaction is more common. In 1954, for example, a royal commission concluded that the crofting system deserved to be maintained if only for the reason that it supported 'a free and independent way of life which in a civilization predominantly urban and industrial in character is worth preserving for its own intrinsic quality'. And in the last twenty years that opinion has gained a growing number of adherents, a development accompanied by a radical revision of the crofter's popular image. To the nineteenth-century advocate of industry and empire the crofter was an idle feckless fellow whose difficulties were largely of his own making – 'the natural fruits' of his own 'indolence and ignorance', as one writer put it. In the increasingly congested and polluted environment of urban Britain in the 1970s, on the other hand, the crofter is frequently idealised, his way of life romanticised, and the region in which he lives depicted as a placid pastoral haven in an ever more frantic world.

The Highlands of the tourist brochure and the holiday cottage are not, however, the Highlands of the crofter. The crofter has never been immune from the pressures generated by capitalist civilization. Indeed he has suffered from them more than most. And today, as the effects of a rapidly expanding tourist trade are supplemented by the consequences of oil-related industrialisation, such pressures are stronger than ever. The crofting tenant is no longer threatened with starvation when his crops fail or when the herring shoals do not materialise. And when his land is expropriated the process is more subtle and less violent than it once was. But the uncertainties of the crofter's day to day existence are nonetheless real and worrying. He has still to work hard for a meagre return. His holding is almost invariably small; his land often poor; his financial resources far from ample. His life, the crofter would agree, has its compensations. That is why he does not abandon it. But his independence is often more apparent than real, while such freedom as he does enjoy is purchased at a price which few of his urban admirers would be willing to pay. The crofter is consequently entitled to respect, not as a quaint anachronism who lives closer to Nature's bosom than the rest of us, but as one of that large majority of mankind which, in the face of immense difficulties, still wins a part of its living by its own efforts from the land.

The photograph on p. 25 surveys the inhospitable eastern shores of Harris in the Outer Hebrides. This land is formed of some of the oldest and hardest rock in the world, named by geologists the 'Lewisian gneiss' after the northern part of the same island. The white sand beaches and *machair* (pasture on lime-rich shell sand) of the western seaboard may be seen in the distance. As James Hunter tells us:

> *In the 1820s and 1830s … the relatively fertile machair lands on the Atlantic coast of Harris were completely cleared and the evicted population settled on the island's bare and rocky east coast, a district where, as a Harris crofter bitterly remarked, 'beasts could not live'.*

The 'Highland Clearances' in which, during the nineteenth century, people were removed by landowners to make way for the more profitable sheep, eventually created such a scandal that legislation, the Crofters' Act of 1886, was introduced to prevent some of the worst abuses and to ensure security of tenure by crofters, although it by no means solved the land problem.

Page 31 shows a view from offshore of the crofting township of Geary on the Vaternish peninsula of the Isle of Skye. A ruined settlement built on the old *clachan* (small village) pattern may be seen in the centre of the photograph. This has been superseded, in the nineteenth century, by a more formal pattern of houses and fields with straight boundaries between them. Donald MacCallum, the young and radical Church of Scotland minister of Vaternish at the height of the land reform troubles in Skye, was one of the leaders of the Highland Land Law Reform Association, and was imprisoned for his part in its activities in 1886, although the vast majority of Protestant clergy of the time formed what the *Oban Times* called an 'unholy alliance' against the land reformers.

Nineteenth-century crofting patterns may also be seen on pp. 28 and 29, both photographs of Lewis in the Outer Hebrides. Peat is still an important fuel in Lewis, and the tradition of going to the 'shieling' to cut peats for use on the fire is still an active one, as the view on p. 27 demonstrates.

A fish farm, a more recent addition to the West Highland landscape, may be seen in the bay – really too enclosed to be an ideal site – in the foreground of the photograph on p. 25.

Fish farming has successfully emerged on the Scottish scene in a very short space of time, and a hundred-fold increase in output has been predicted for the decade ending 1990. Both the sustained development of the industry and the protection of this hitherto little-disturbed coastline, internationally renowned for its scenic and nature conservation qualities, are dependent upon an extremely careful integration of the development into the marine environment.

PART THREE
THE 'GOLDEN EMBLEM'

Perhaps even more nostalgic than the crofting landscapes in the previous part are those in which life is not quite so harsh as that of the crofter, but nevertheless retains both a strong daily connection with the land or the sea, and also relative independence in a context of co-operation. Again, the romance of these apparently balanced and harmonious landscapes is partly real, partly imagined, but exercises a strong influence on twentieth-century Scottish consciousness. This influence, together with the growing concern for wild landscapes, may lead us to find ways of dealing with some of the problems that we have created for ourselves and for the other inhabitants with whom we share the land.

Page 38 shows what is perhaps one of the most romantic and picturesque of Scottish scenes, the vista from Bemersyde, near Melrose in the Borders, towards the Eildon Hills and the River Tweed. It is known as 'Scott's View', as it was a great favourite of Sir Walter Scott, who lived nearby at Abbotsford on the Tweed.

Romance also attaches to Traprain Law in East Lothian, the hill shown in the photograph on pp. 40-1. A volcanic outcrop left standing proud of the surrounding ice-eroded landscape of softer sedimentary rocks, the hill has a history of several thousand years of human settlement, and is known for the discovery there of a buried hoard of Roman silver, now in the collections of the National Museums of Scotland in Edinburgh. The small red dots on the skyline of the hill are warning notices placed on the edge of a deep quarry, now no longer active, which has removed much of the far side of the hill.

A man-made landscape which is nevertheless, unexpectedly perhaps, a balanced one with a good representation of wildlife as well as human activity is the heather moorland of the Lammermuir Hills, shown on p. 43. The striking patterns are caused by successive years of burning of the moorland in

113

patches for grouse and sheep management. The most recently burned areas show up clearly because of the intense black of the charred heather stems. Such moorland must be managed with care, as too frequent burning is destructive, and too infrequent burning allows the take-over of tall heather, which chokes plants of other species.

On p. 42 is a photograph of Stromness, an Orcadian town built to a Scandinavian pattern, with the gable-ends of the buildings facing on to the sea, an arrangement unusual in Scotland. This way of structuring the sea-front of the town gives all the householders easy access to the sea and to their boats which are, or were, kept immediately adjacent to the houses. Stromness was the last port of call for ships going on the North Atlantic route to North America and Greenland, and had a long association with the Hudson's Bay Company and with commercial whaling in the Greenland Sea. Herring fishing also boomed here, as elsewhere, around the turn of the nineteenth century, although oil-related business activities and tourism have now become more important.

PART FOUR

CAVES OF GUILT... PINNACLES OF JUBILATION

A city, symbolically understood, is the environment which imagination creates for itself... First and last, we inhabit a myth...

Kathleen Raine, 'On the Mythological' in *Defending Ancient Springs*

Page 47 shows Edinburgh in its romantic guise as the archetypal small city. Its topography and situation ideally fit it to occupy such a role in the imagination, although certain of its prominent buildings may not accord too well with a present-day view of the essential components of the 'ideal city'. Edinburgh Castle, which dates back to the eleventh century, and the adjacent medieval 'Old Town' in the foreground of the photograph, were built on a 'crag-and-tail' feature of hard volcanic rock left standing above the surrounding landscape by retreating ice-sheets, in a similar way to Traprain Law on pp. 40-1. By the eighteenth century overcrowding in the Old Town was extreme, and the Georgian 'New Town', an area of more spacious streets and gardens seen in the background of the picture, was established on the north side of the hollow now forming Princes Street Gardens, once a loch. Between two parts of the gardens stands the National Gallery of Scotland, shown on p. 53; the railway runs in a tunnel beneath.

Throughout the twentieth century, Scotland has been active in attempts to produce good public ('council') housing available for rent. The Kennyhill and Riddrie Housing Scheme, seen on p. 49, was one of Scotland's first large post-1919 municipal housing estates. The last of the houses were built in 1927 and they all had, as an experiment, cavity walling to prevent damp penetration, as well as electric servicing. The scheme included a school, churches and a library. There is also a bowling green, seen in the centre of the photograph. The scheme is now, unfortunately, closely passed by the extremely busy M8 motorway between Edinburgh and Glasgow, seen at the bottom of the picture.

More recent housing, and an associated play area, is shown on pp. 50-1, at Craigmillar in Edinburgh. To the right of the playground figure, in a gap between the houses, can be seen a triangular form which is catching the light. This is a bonfire assembled by local children to celebrate Guy Fawkes' Day on the fifth of November. The photographs were taken on the day before the bonfire was due to be lit, when the traditional heap of old furniture and wood had reached its highest extent.

Although many municipal housing initiatives are now perceived to have failed to realize the aims of their builders, the will towards social justice for all remains a political priority in Scotland.

PART FIVE

A HEAVEN ON EARTH

The photograph on p. 62 shows one of the most extensive and dramatic formal gardens in Scotland, at Drummond Castle in Perthshire. The gardens were first laid out in 1630 to a French design, and landscaped again around 1830 in the design of the Scottish flag, the St Andrew's Cross. At the central point upon which all the paths converge stands an obelisk in the form of a sundial, which has approximately fifty faces for telling the time in most of the capital cities in Europe.

Opinions on the virtues of such gardens vary. The two ends of the spectrum might be represented by the two quotations below:

Fundamentally, all gardening is the transference of a vision into a touchable and seeable reality. It may be a re-creation on earth of the garden from which man came, or an anticipation of the paradise to which, if he behaves himself, he will eventually journey.

Miles and John Hadfield, *Gardens of Delight*

*Grove nods at grove, each alley has a
    brother
And half the platform just reflects the other.
The suffering eye inverted nature sees,
Trees cut to statues, statues thick as trees;*

Alexander Pope, *Epistle to Burlington*

Whatever the merits or demerits of the planting of extensive parks and gardens, such enterprises require considerable sums of money for their making and upkeep. Even a small private 'paradise', such as the grounds of St Michael's House, the mill-owner's mansion at Inveresk shown on p. 63, represents part of the considerable profits from the labour of the many workers in the mill. Also shown in the photograph is part of Brunton's Wireworks, and the graveyard of St Michael's, Inveresk.

Many large houses, such as St Michael's House, and Tyninghame House, seen on p. 60, have now been divided into separate flats. Financial pressures have also resulted in the commercial exploitation of mature parkland trees, as at Tyninghame, although on that estate at least these will be replanted.

The Royal Botanic Garden in Edinburgh, shown under snow on p. 59, forms a wonderful recreational area for the people of Edinburgh (although only until dusk!), as well as being an important research establishment with links all over the world. An arboretum such as that shown here inevitably appears to be a rather strange kind of wood, as inhabitants of every continent are represented in it, and almost every tree is of a different species from every other.

PART SIX

AND THE MACHINES SAY...

The products of industry and an efficient network of communications are apparently essential features of modern life, and have now reached almost every part of Scotland. The stories of the building of such structures as lighthouses and railways are often impressive tales of initiative and endurance bordering on heroism. The exploits of the Victorian builders of the West Highland Railway, and especially its Rannoch Moor section (shown on p. 67), for instance, deserve our greatest respect. A quotation from a contemporary account in the *Glasgow Evening News* of 11 August 1894, on the opening of the West Highland Railway, sums up one approach to the project:

All who have the interest of our Highland population at heart will join in hoping that a brighter day has dawned for them, and that with the breaking down of the natural barriers which have so long confined them, there will follow an era of prosperity of which parallels can be found wherever the railway has found an entrance.

Glasgow Evening News

But note the date upon which the railway was opened. The twelfth of August (the 'Glorious Twelfth') is the beginning of the grouse-shooting season, when southern gentlemen annually arrive in droves in the Highlands of Scotland to pursue their chosen pastime.

Roads, as well as railways, have for many people an eternal fascination, conjured up by the archetypal Scottish travel addict, Robert Louis Stevenson, writing in *Travels with a Donkey*:

For my part, I travel not to go anywhere, but to go. I travel for travel's sake. The great affair is to move.

Many people may now feel, however, that their relationship with roads and the internal combustion engine is at best a love-hate one, better captured by the words of the Orcadian poet Edwin Muir in another context:

*The endless trap lay everywhere,
And all the roads ran in a maze
Hither and thither, like a web
To catch the careless days.*

'The Escape'

Such an apparently inescapable network of roads may be seen on p. 72, the much praised segregated traffic/pedestrian system at Cumbernauld New Town. Cumbernauld, designated as a New Town in 1956, and situated between Glasgow and Edinburgh in an exposed hilltop position, may well have looked better on the planner's drawing board than it does to a lone pedestrian on a cold and windy day in the depths of winter. It is nevertheless internationally renowned for (Modernist) architectural and planning concepts, winning awards for community architecture in the 1960s.

Massive construction projects such as road-building have other environmental consequences in locations geographically separate from the situation of the projects themselves. One of these is shown on p. 69, a distant view of the pilot operations for the rock-crushing plant at Glensanda 'superquarry' at its 'remote', deep-water site on the shores of Loch Linnhe. The quarry was opened by a Somerset-based company in response to an identified deficit situation in roadstone in the south-east of England, as a long-term source of granite rock for general purpose construction aggregate. The pilot stage had, when this photograph was taken, produced approximately three million tonnes of material, most of which has been

exported. The quarry, which is programmed to be the largest in the world by the mid-1990s, is projected to produce up to 7.5 million tonnes of crushed rock *per annum* once it is fully operational, for removal in bulk carriers by sea. Approximately one-third of its production is destined for the eastern seaboard of the USA, one-third for the English Channel Tunnel operations, and the remaining third for other uses in the south-east of England. The quarry will employ approximately 200 people. As Glensanda is situated in a scenically beautiful area where conventional quarry practices would be unacceptable, the company is attempting to minimize environmental impact by the use of innovative techniques. Company director David Yeoman is nevertheless on record (*New Civil Engineer*, 6 April 1989) as saying:

No major quarries have been opened up in the south-east [of England] since the 1970s... [because] planning constraints are so severe... No matter how sensitively you develop a quarry it is an antisocial business. We specifically wanted a secluded site and I see this type of superquarry as the way forward in future.

The large-scale exploitation of the natural resources of the west coast of Scotland as a relatively cheap source of raw materials for distant entrepreneurs is not new; it might indeed even have become an established tradition. In the nineteenth century Jesse Hartley, the civil engineer in charge of the massive reconstruction of Liverpool docks, a larger-than-life character variously described as artist and despot, opened and operated a granite quarry in Kirkcudbrightshire to provide the stone he required for the dockyard works. In the eighteenth century, as W. Ivison Macadam tells us:

After the rebellion of 1715 the Highlands were placed under military regulation, and an opening was presented for English enterprise. No scruples were then expressed as to the waste of timber, and the Scottish forests were extensively used for the conversion of English ore. The ore, being heavy and compact, was more easily transported to the wood than the timber to the ore.

(In the seventeenth century, '. . . the manufacture of iron with wood charcoal had so far exhausted the forests of England that various Acts of Parliament were passed for their protection.')

A more sustainable resource, the water power of the Falls of Clyde, just south of the old county town of Lanark, was harnessed by the Glasgow entrepreneur David Dale, originally in partnership with the Englishman Richard Arkwright, the inventor of mechanized cotton

spinning, in his early industrial development named New Lanark, begun in 1785. New Lanark, seen on p. 68, is today the pre-eminent example of a cotton-spinning village from the first period of Britain's industrialization, and has been very little changed physically since its building. David Dale, and his better-known son-in-law, the Welshman Robert Owen, author of the set of essays entitled *A New View of Society, or Essays on the Principle of the Formation of Character*, were innovative and relatively enlightened employers. They developed and implemented ideas on education, social reform and systems of economic organization which were very advanced for the times, and which exert a continuing influence on our thinking on these matters today.

Atmospheric pollution, which is an inevitable side-effect of most industrial activity to some degree, is made more obvious, as shown on p. 73 (taken above Grangemouth, the first deep-sea container port in the UK) by the weather conditions accompanying a 'temperature inversion'. This situation is often associated with an area of high atmospheric pressure, giving rise to the so-called 'anti-cyclonic gloom' which is a feature of many industrial areas. Under normal atmospheric conditions, the air temperature decreases with height above the ground. When a temperature inversion exists in the atmosphere, however, a layer of warmer air is found *above* a layer of colder air, and this stable situation effectively traps fumes which would otherwise be dispersed. The Forth estuary does not always look like this, but the photograph graphically demonstrates the scale of the problem.

PART SEVEN
THE FURROW DRAWN BY ADAM'S FINGER

Attitudes to various agricultural and forestry activities have recently become another focus for debate on land issues in Scotland, although many of the features of this debate are not new. The advantages of 'agricultural improvement' (field drainage, crop rotation and the introduction of new varieties of plants and animals, together with methods of 'scientific' husbandry) are obviously of benefit to all who live in a modern Western society: time saved, better conditions for the human, if not the animal – in many cases, certainly not the animal – workforce, higher yielding crops, as T.C. Smout has pointed out:

In Scotland in 1840 it took 22 man days a year to tend an acre of barley; by 1914 it was down to 12, and by 1958, to only 3.

A Century of the Scottish People, 1830–1950

The penalties to be paid for these benefits, however, have long been recognized, even by a man such as Robert Burns, who died young, probably largely because his health had been undermined at an early age by unavoidable and excessively heavy manual work for a boy of his years on the 'unimproved' and difficult farms in Ayrshire where his family struggled to make a living. His views, recorded in his diary of a visit to the Lothians and Berwickshire in 1787, when 'improvement' was well advanced in those counties compared with the situation in Ayrshire, show us his doubts (although it has been suggested that this passage is apocryphal):

Linlithgow – a fertile improved country – West Lothian. The more elegance and luxury among the farms, I always observe, in equal proportion, the rudeness and stupidity of the peasantry. This remark I have made all over the Lothians, Merse, Roxburgh, etc. For this, among other reasons, I think that a man of romantic taste, a 'Man of Feeling', will be better pleased with the poverty, but intelligent minds of the peasantry in Ayrshire (peasantry they are all below the Justice of Peace), than the opulence of a club of Merse farmers, when at the same time he considers the vandalism of their plough-folks, etc. I carry this idea so far, that an unenclosed, half-improven country is to me actually more agreeable, and gives me more pleasure as a prospect, than a country cultivated like a garden.

Lewis Grassic Gibbon, in his series of novels *A Scots Quair*, most notably in *Sunset Song*, also voices his strong reservations:

It was the old Scotland that perished then . . . we are told that great machines come soon to till the land, and the great herds come to feed on it, the crofter has gone, the man with the house and the steading of his own and the land closer to his heart than the flesh of his body.

Pages 75-7 show modern agricultural landscapes where wild nature, even in the form of hedgerows and small patches of woodland, has been almost entirely eliminated, to the improvement of crop yields, but to the detriment of the richness and balance of the environment.

The photographs on pp. 76 and 77, both showing fields of oilseed rape (*Brassica napus*), a relatively 'new' crop to appear on the Scottish agricultural scene, demonstrate some of the economic, rather than physical, mechanisms

at work today which are bringing about agricultural change. A dramatic expansion of the acreage of oilseed rape grown in the UK, amounting to what has been described as a 'yellow revolution', has taken place since Britain's entry into the European Economic Community in 1970. This has been the result of two main factors: first, the intrinsic value of rape as a break-crop in intensive cereal crop rotation and, second, the financial support provided for the crop under the Common Agricultural Policy of the EEC. This 'yellow revolution', which arrived in Scotland in 1979–80, and which has been the subject of considerable controversy, may well be about to come to an end, however, because of changes in EEC thinking on the present support payment system to farmers, and also because of changes in the development of alternative break-crops, such as linseed, evening primrose and sunflowers.

Commercial forestry practices have also been much criticized recently, especially those which produce large areas of a monoculture of conifers, like that shown in the photograph on p. 82, in which the terrain is so unsuitable for the natural growth of the trees that fertilizer must be sprayed on to them by helicopter to make them at all economic as a crop. Worse still is the situation in the 'Flow Country' of Caithness and Sutherland, where many plantations have been sited in such unsuitable places that the trees do not grow successfully even with the application of fertilizer, as in that shown on p. 83. The events in the Flow Country have been particularly unfortunate because of the associated destruction of a unique habitat of mire and moorland with its wildlife; part of this habitat may be seen at the right of the photograph on p. 83. Once again, artificial economic factors involving subsidies and tax incentives, intended in this case to encourage landowners to plant trees – in itself a good thing – have been the reason for these changes in the landscape. In the Flow Country, and in many other moorland areas of Scotland, these incentives have had unfortunate results, although many absentee shareholders and middlemen have nevertheless received large sums of money from the public purse. This situation provides an excellent example of the pitfalls which threaten attempts to bring about environmental and economic improvement in one area without sufficient consideration of the possible consequences in others.

On p. 85 we see the remains of a forestry plantation in the Great Glen. Two small, square 'high altitude trials' are left standing above the clear-felled rectangular plantation. Above them, the present-day semi-natural vegetation of blanket bog covers the hill-tops – once, the hills would probably have supported native woodland of either pine or oak, before felling and grazing pressures denuded them.

Fortunately, modern forestry is capable of more enlightened practice than that shown in these photographs (see p. 109 and notes to Part Ten). Unfortunately, the proportion of environmentally sensitive plantations is at present still very small.

PART EIGHT
THESE DARKENED FIELDS

The landscape of 'post-industrial wasteland' which is represented throughout Britain appears in various forms in Scotland. Ancient quarrying and mining activity has left its mark, as shown in the photographs on pp. 87-90, although in many other former industrial areas 'tidying-up' operations have been extremely successful, so much so that some industrial remains are now protected as museum sites, for example Lady Victoria Colliery at Newton-grange, now part of the Scottish Mining Museum (see p. 101 in Part Nine).

Page 90 shows a complex combination of landscape features, mostly connected with the coal industry. The area of the Fife coast where this photograph was taken is one which has a long history of coal mining. The ventilation shafts of coal pits, some dating back to the sixteenth century, sometimes emerged from under the sea, as here. Until as late as the eighteenth century, coal miners in Fife and the Lothians were the slaves of the mine-owners. This situation came to an end only in 1799, by which time the industry had expanded so much that a large enough labour force could no longer be obtained locally, even by these methods, and workers from areas outside Scotland, who would not accept such conditions of employment, had also to be engaged. The ruins of a colliery and saltworks, dating from the early nineteenth century, may be seen on what was once an island about a mile offshore in Torry Bay in the Firth of Forth. They are now surrounded by a land 'reclamation' project in which fly-ash from the nearby coal-fired power station at Longannet is being used to fill in a series of artificially created lagoons.

The heavy industries associated with the first Industrial Revolution have now largely vanished from the Scottish landscape. A few shipyards on the River Clyde, such as those shown on p. 92 (photographed in 1986), still remain operational; some of the new purposes to which the 'bonny banks o' Clyde' have recently been put are shown on p. 103 in Part Nine.

More sinister remains tend to be associated with the two World Wars, the Orkney Islands being an area where many of these are still visible, as shown on pp. 93 and 94. The wreck of the British warship HMS *Royal Oak*, torpedoed and sunk in 1939 with the loss of more than 800 lives, lies in Scapa Flow in 30 metres of water, and can be seen from the air when the sea is calm. Many of the dead still lie within the hull of the ship, which is an officially designated war cemetery. Oil still escapes continually from the wreck, and can be clearly seen forming a long slick on the surface of the sea, at the bottom of the photograph on p. 94, a chilling reminder of the tragedy.

The Iron Age hillfort in the foreground of the photograph on p. 95 is probably more than 2,000 years old. The traces on the landscape of ramparts such as these – whether they were built for truly defensive reasons or merely as a display of martial panoply is debated among archaeologists – can easily be removed by later tenants of the site if they so choose. The remains of some monuments of the Nuclear Age, however, such as the nuclear power station at Torness seen in the background of the picture, are likely to cause coming generations considerably more difficulties, and for far longer into the future than the Iron Age is into the past. The twentieth century has discovered the secrets of the creation of the most fundamental, and possibly the ultimate, form of poison, without as yet discovering the antidote.

PART NINE
MAN-INFECTED, MAN-PROTECTED

Where visitors enjoying recreation in the countryside or by the sea (as shown on pp. 98, 99 and in Part Ten, on pp. 107 and 110-11) are few in relation to their surroundings, all is well. This situation is, however, becoming rarer in Scotland today. As already mentioned in the notes to Part One, one of the largest areas of semi-natural land in Scotland, the Cairngorm Mountains, is increasingly under pressure, from the activities of skiers in particular (see p. 97).

Communities of all kinds, built around living industries – from fishing villages in areas such as the East Neuk of Fife (p. 100) to mining towns such as that until recently associated with an active coal mine, Lady Victoria Colliery at Newtongrange, now part of the Scottish Mining Museum (p. 101) – are turning to tourism and the 'heritage industry' in some form as their main activities. This is yet another aspect of the environment where a balance must be struck between change and conservation. Museums and preserved monuments are obviously an important part of understanding the past, but it is debatable, and increasingly debated, whether it is desirable to attempt to preserve human environments without the activities which gave them life, thus presenting a misleading idea to contemporary visitors of the character of the lives once lived there. Skilled interpretation is a necessary, although often insufficient, adjunct to any such attempt.

The leisure industry and consumerism increasingly go hand in hand, as can be seen on pp. 102 and 104. The site of the 1988 Glasgow Garden Festival is shown on p. 103. Subsequent re-development of the area as a housing estate has taken place without, as might have been expected, the preservation of the trees and gardens established, albeit rather hastily perhaps, for the Festival itself. The centre of Glasgow is nevertheless undergoing a renaissance commercially and physically, and it will be interesting to see how this attempt at a new townscape develops in the future.

PART TEN
EARTH WAS THE ONLY MEETING PLACE

New human attitudes to our relationship to the environment are desperately needed. This has long been recognized by a few people, both within and outwith the scientific community, and is now increasingly recognized by many. The four photographs in this final part explore some aspects of what such new attitudes might involve.

Page 108 shows the summit of Calton Hill in Edinburgh during the Edinburgh International Festival of 1987. The incised white, temporary, 'land-art' symbols of contemporary artist Kate Whiteford, suggestive of ancient world views and of values traditionally associated with the 'feminine', largely in eclipse in present-day Western society, appear among some rather more permanent monuments associated with traditionally 'masculine', 'rational' values: the City Observatory, the Nelson Monument (built in 1807 in the form of a telescope), and a building intended to resemble the Parthenon, planned as the Scottish National War Memorial to the dead in the Napoleonic Wars, and never completed.

The ideal cultivated rural landscape has been described as a 'holey blanket', in which farming and forestry are carried out together, and provision for wildlife habitats and places for other human activities is incorporated into the thinking behind the design. (It is important for us to realize that all such 'unnatural' landscapes are in fact 'designed', and continually re-designed, sometimes unconsciously, and often by default, by their human inhabitants, although the design process may sometimes take place over hundreds, or even thousands, of years.) Landscapes such as that shown on p. 109, showing integrated farming and forestry near Selkirk in the Borders, go some way towards this ideal, although very few broad-leaved trees have been planted here, and 'farm forestry' as it is ideally envisaged by its advocates has not yet really made an appearance in Britain. This landscape is, nevertheless, one which clearly shows that it is both cared about and cared for. Healthy, living landscapes result from the integration of rational with feeling values.

Hic quem creticus edit Dedalus est Laberinthus
de quo nullus vadere quivit qui fuit intus
ni Theseus gratis Ariadne stamine iutus.

(This is the labyrinth which the Cretan Daedalus built, out of which nobody can find his way except Theseus, nor could he have done it unless he had been helped by Ariadne's thread, for love.)

Inscription from the porch of cathedral at Lucca in Italy, quoted in *The Geography of the Imagination* by Guy Davenport.

Patricia Macdonald, April 1989

FURTHER READING

PART ONE

BAIRD, W.J., *The Scenery of Scotland: The Structure Beneath*, Edinburgh, National Museums of Scotland, 1988.

BUNCE, R.G.H. and JEFFERS, J.H.R., *The Native Pinewoods of Scotland*, Cambridge, Institute of Terrestrial Ecology, 1977.

BURNETT, J.H., ed., *The Vegetation of Scotland*, Edinburgh, Oliver and Boyd, 1964.

DAVENPORT, GUY, *The Geography of the Imagination*, London, Pan Books (Picador), 1984.

MEIER, C.A., *A Testament to the Wilderness: Ten Essays on an address by C.A. Meier* (presented at the Third World Wilderness Congress in Inverness, 1983), Zurich, Daimon Verlag/Santa Monica, Lapis Press, 1985.

MUIR, JOHN, *My First Summer in the Sierra*, Edinburgh, Canongate, 1988.

NATURE CONSERVANCY COUNCIL, *Nature Conservation in Great Britain*, Shrewsbury, Nature Conservancy Council, 1984.

RAINE, KATHLEEN, *Collected Poems*, London, Allen & Unwin, 1981.

RATCLIFFE, D.A., ed., *A Nature Conservation Review*, Cambridge, Cambridge University Press for National Environment Research Council and Nature Conservancy Council, 1977.

STEVEN, H.M. and CARLISLE, A., *The Native Pinewoods of Scotland*, Edinburgh, Oliver and Boyd, 1959.

STONE, CHRISTOPHER, *Should Trees Have Standing? Towards legal rights for natural objects*, Los Altos, William Kaufmann Inc., 1974.

WHITTOW, J.B., *Geology and Scenery in Scotland*, Harmondsworth, Penguin Books, 1977.

YEATS, WILLIAM BUTLER, *Collected Poems*, London, Macmillan, 1958.

PART TWO

BOTTING, DOUGLAS, *Wilderness Europe (The World's Wild Places)*, Amsterdam, Time Life International, 1976.

DAVENPORT, GUY, *op. cit.*

GOTO, JOHN and HORSEFIELD, CRAIGIE, 'Terezin' in *Of Memory*, Creative Camera, 1/1989, pp.25–31.

HARRIS, MARVIN, *Cannibals and Kings: the Origins of Cultures*, London, Fontana, 1978.

HUNTER, JAMES, *The Making of the Crofting Community*, Edinburgh, John Donald, 1976.

MacCAIG, NORMAN, *Voice Over*, London, Chatto & Windus, 1988.

MacKENZIE, ALEXANDER, *The History of the Highland Clearances*, Melven Press, 1986.

MacLEAN, MALCOLM and CARRELL, CHRISTOPHER, eds, *As an Fhearann (From the Land): Clearance, Conflict and Crofting*, Edinburgh, Mainstream/Stornoway, An Lanntair/Glasgow, Third Eye Centre, 1986.

MARSHALL, ROSALIND, *Mary, Queen of Scots*, Edinburgh, HMSO, 1988.

NATURE CONSERVANCY COUNCIL, *Fishfarming and the Safeguard of the Natural Marine Environment of Scotland*, Edinburgh, Nature Conservancy Council, 1989.

PREBBLE, JOHN, *The Highland Clearances*, London, Secker & Warburg, 1963/ Harmondsworth, Penguin Books, 1969.

SMOUT, T.C., *A History of the Scottish People, 1560–1830*, London and Glasgow, Collins, 1969.

PART THREE

BRANDT, BILL and HAWORTH-BOOTH, MARK, eds, *The Land: Twentieth Century Landscape Photographs selected by Bill Brandt*, London, Gordon Fraser, 1985.

DRABBLE, MARGARET and LEWINSKI, JORGE, *A Writer's Britain: Landscape in Literature*, London, Thames and Hudson, 1979.

FENTON, ALEXANDER, *Scottish Country Life*, Edinburgh, John Donald, 1976.

HAY, GEORGE CAMPBELL and MacALISTER, ARCHIE, *Seeker-Reaper*, Edinburgh, Saltire Society, 1988.

MacCAIG, NORMAN, *Collected Poems*, London, Chatto & Windus, 1988.

MacLEAN, CHARLES, *The Fringe of Gold: The Fishing Villages of Scotland's East Coast, Orkney and Shetland*, Edinburgh, Canongate, 1985.

MELLOR, DAVID, ed., *A Paradise Lost: The Neo-Romantic Imagination in Britain, 1935–55*, London, Lund Humphries/Barbican Art Gallery, 1987.

SIMPSON, ANN, *Paul Nash: Landscape of the Vernal Equinox (A closer look at painters and paintings 5)*, Edinburgh, National Galleries of Scotland, 1987.

PART FOUR

NORBERG-SCHULZ, CHRISTIAN, *Genius Loci: Towards a Phenomenology of Architecture*, London, Academy, 1980.

RAINE, KATHLEEN, 'On the Mythological' in *Defending Ancient Springs*, Ipswich, Golgonooza, 1985.

SMOUT, T.C., *A History of the Scottish People, 1560–1830*, London and Glasgow, Collins, 1969.

SMOUT, T.C., *A Century of the Scottish People, 1830–1950*, London and Glasgow, Collins, 1986.

YOUNGSON, A.J., *The Making of Classical Edinburgh, 1750–1840*, Edinburgh, Edinburgh University Press, 1966.

PART FIVE

FOWLES, JOHN, *The Tree*, London, Aurum Press, 1979/New York, Ecco Press, 1983.

HADFIELD, MILES and JOHN, *Gardens of Delight*, London, Cassell, 1964.

LITTLE, G. ALLAN, *Scotland's Gardens*, Edinburgh, Spur Books, 1981.

MIDDA, SARA, *In and Out of the Garden*, London, Sidgwick and Jackson, 1981.

MILTON, JOHN, *Paradise Lost (The Poetical Works of John Milton)*, London, Macmillan, 1905.

TAIT, A. A., *The Landscape Garden in Scotland, 1735–1835*, Edinburgh, Edinburgh University Press, 1980.

THACKER, CHRISTOPHER, *The History of Gardens*, London, Croom Helm, 1979.

PART SIX

ALLEN, NIC, *David Dale, Robert Owen and the Story of New Lanark*, Edinburgh, Moubray House Press/New Lanark, New Lanark Conservation, 1986.

ANDREWS, CYRIL BRUYN, *The Railway Age*, London, *Country Life*, 1937.

ANG, TOM and POLLARD, MICHAEL, *Walking the Scottish Highlands: General Wade's Military Roads*, London, André Deutsch, 1984.

BAYNES, KEN and ROBINSON, ALAN, *Work: Art and Society Two*, London, Lund Humphries/Welsh Arts Council, 1970.

HAYWARD, DAVID, 'Moor Granite', *New Civil Engineer*, 6 April 1989, pp. 35–9.

MACADAM, W. IVISON, *Notes on the Ancient Iron Industry in Scotland*, Proceedings of the Society of Antiquaries of Scotland, 1886, pp. 89–131.

MUIR, EDWIN, *Collected Poems*, London, Faber & Faber, 1963.

RITCHIE NOAKES, NANCY, *Jesse Hartley, Dock Engineer to the Port of Liverpool, 1824–60*, Liverpool, Merseyside County Council/Merseyside County Museums, 1980.

THOMAS, JOHN, *The West Highland Railway*, London, Pan Books, 1970.

THOMAS, R. S., *Experimenting with an Amen*, London, Macmillan, 1986.

PART SEVEN

BOCKEMÜHL, JOCHEN, *Dying Forests: a crisis in consciousness*, Stroud, Hawthorn Press, 1986.

DRABBLE, MARGARET and LEWINSKI, JORGE, *op. cit.*

GRASSIC GIBBON, LEWIS, *Sunset Song (A Scots Quair)*, London, Hutchinson, 1946.

LOCKHART, J. G., *Life of Burns*, London, 1828.

MUIR, EDWIN, *op. cit.*

ROBINSON, GUY, *Agricultural Change*, Edinburgh, N B Publications, 1988.

SMOUT, T. C., *A Century of the Scottish People, 1830–1950*, London and Glasgow, Collins, 1986.

SPROTT, GAVIN, *Robert Burns, Farmer*, Edinburgh, National Museums of Scotland, 1989.

PART EIGHT

BAYNES, KEN, *War: Art and Society One*, London, Lund Humphries/Welsh Arts Council, 1970.

DAVIES, JOHN, *A Green and Pleasant Land*, Manchester, Cornerhouse, 1987.

DUCKHAM, BARON F., *A History of the Scottish Coal Industry, Vol. 1: 1700–1815*, Newton Abbot, David & Charles, 1970.

MUIR, EDWIN, *op. cit.*

SCHEI, LIV KJÖRSVIK and MOBERG, GUNNIE, *The Orkney Story*, London, Batsford, 1985.

PART NINE

CONROY, J. W. H., WATSON, ADAM and GUNSON, R., eds, *Conference on Conservation of the Cairngorms*, Institute of Terrestrial Ecology/Highlands and Islands Development Board/Nature Conservancy Council, 1989.

CRIMP, DOUGLAS, 'On the Museum's Ruins' in FOSTER, HAL, ed., *Postmodern Culture*, London, Pluto Press, 1984.

CURRY-LINDAHL, KAI, WATSON, ADAM and WATSON, R. DRENNAN, *The Future of the Cairngorms*, Aberdeen, The North East Mountain Trust, 1982.

DAVIES, JOHN, *op. cit.*

HORNE, DONALD, *The Great Museum*, London, Pluto Press, 1984.

MUNRO, ROBIN, 'Hills' in BROWN, HAMISH, ed., *Poems of the Scottish Hills*, Aberdeen, Aberdeen University Press, 1982.

SCOTTISH MUSEUMS COUNCIL, *Museums are for People*, Edinburgh, HMSO for Scottish Museums Council, 1985.

SMITH, ROGER and CRUMLEY, JIM, *Cairngorms at the Crossroads*, Edinburgh, Scottish Wild Land Group, 1987.

PART TEN

ALEXANDER, CHRISTOPHER, *The Timeless Way of Building*, New York, Oxford University Press, 1979.

BOCKEMÜHL, JOCHEN, *op. cit.*

CAPRA, FRITJOF, *The Turning Point: Science, Society and the Rising Culture*, London, Wildwood House, 1982/London, Fontana (Flamingo), 1983.

CHURCH OF SCOTLAND, Society, Religion and Technology Project: *While the Earth Endures: A Report on the Theological and Ethical Considerations of Responsible Land Use*, Edinburgh, Quorum Press, 1986.

COOPER, THOMAS JOSHUA, *Dreaming the Gokstadt: Northern Lands and Islands*, Edinburgh, Graeme Murray, 1988.

DAVENPORT, GUY, *op. cit.*

DURRELL, LAWRENCE, *A Smile in the Mind's Eye*, London, Wildwood House, 1980.

FERGUSON, MARILYN, *The Aquarian Conspiracy*, London, Routledge, 1981/London, Granada (Paladin), 1982.

FRASER DARLING, FRANK, *Wilderness and Plenty (The Reith Lectures 1969)*, London, Ballantine/Friends of the Earth, 1971.

LOVELOCK, J. E., *Gaia: A New Look at Life on Earth*, Oxford, Oxford University Press, 1979.

MERCHANT, CAROLYN, *The Death of Nature*, Harper & Row, 1980.

MUIR, EDWIN, *op. cit.*

RAINE, KATHLEEN, 'On the Symbol' in *Defending Ancient Springs*, Ipswich, Golgonooza, 1985.

STRACHAN, ELSPETH and GORDON, *Freeing the Feminine*, Dunbar, Labarum, 1985.

TOBIAS, MICHAEL CHARLES and DRASDO, HAROLD, eds, *The Mountain Spirit*, London, Gollancz, 1980.

TREVELYAN, GEORGE, *Magic Casements: The Use of Poetry in the Expanding of Consciousness*, London, Coventure, 1980.

WARD, BARBARA, *Progress for a Small Planet*, Harmondsworth, Penguin Books, 1979.

ACKNOWLEDGEMENTS

A great many people and organizations have very kindly given me advice, information, help and support during the making of this book and of the photographs. I should like to thank particularly the following:

For generous help with specialist information, the staff of the British Geological Survey, especially Tom Bain, Nigel Fannin, Richard Gillanders and Graham Smith; Laurie Campbell, wildlife photographer; Isobel Cameron, Bob Jones and Mr Paterson of the Forestry Commission; Duncan Campbell and John Mackay of the Countryside Commission for Scotland; Debbie Mays of Historic Buildings and Monuments, Scotland; Jim Conroy of the Institute of Terrestrial Ecology; Bill Baird, Ian Bunyan, Jenni Calder, Hugh Cheape, Ian Larner, Harry Macpherson, Bob Reekie, Gavin Sprott and Jim Wood of the National Museums of Scotland; Rawdon Goodier, Murray Ferguson and Mike Matthew of the Nature Conservancy Council; Elizabeth Williamson of Penguin Books; John Hunt of the Royal Society for the Protection of Birds; and David Sugden of the University of Edinburgh. For his enthusiastic and effective support of our aerial photography, Aubrey Manning of the University of Edinburgh.

For help on the flying side, Harald Vox, whose enthusiasm for flying was highly significant; my inspired, understanding and long-suffering chief flying instructor Paul Hewett and his team at Edinburgh Flying Club; Dave Andrews who ensured that I passed my written examinations; Gerry Chamberlain for lots of encouragement (and those perfectly timed gentians); Kathy Burnham, Carol Jones, Keith and Karen Rice, Mike and Win Vickers and Gordon and Dot Webb of CSE Aviation, Oxford, for their hospitality and friendship and for their dedicated and irreplaceable further training of my photographic pilot, Angus Macdonald and myself; Thea and Naki Doniach and Patricia Moss for their generous initiation into the secrets of island life between flights at Oxford; Jane Dalgleish and Laure Paterson, very special flying friends; and the staff of Edinburgh Air Centre, especially Peter Howard-Johnston and George Lamb, for their valiant efforts to keep us and our cameras in the air.

For help on many different aspects of photography: my father, Walter Scott, in whose darkroom I was first introduced to the magical qualities of the medium; my mother, Mazoura Scott, for the deeply-felt involvement with poetry and pictures which she communicated to me, and for her very helpful responses to specific photographs; very special thanks to Thomas Joshua Cooper for his generously given and invaluable advice, enthusiasm and understanding and for the unique learning experience made possible by him at the Photography Workshop landscape course at Hospitalfield, together with Willie Payne and all the photographer participants; Kim Allen, Alastair Hunter and Les Stevens, from whose generous professional advice and friendship I have learned a great deal; James Simpson for his support and for many stimulating discussions and exchanges of ideas; Lindsey Prentiss for her understanding friendship and reliably honest advice on work in progress over many years; Stephen Dalton and Tim Harris of the Natural History Photographic Agency, Murray and Kate Johnston of Scottish Photographic Works and Peter Scott for support and advice; for support on the exhibition side: Aase and Peter Goldsmith of the Corridor Gallery, Glenrothes; Clara Young of Dundee Art Gallery, with Colin Ruscoe; Edinburgh District Council; William Wilson of Lyth Arts Centre, with Katriana Hazell; Vicky Molyneux and Ali Jack; the National Museums of Scotland; the staff of The Photographers' Gallery, London, especially David Chandler, Martin Caiger-Smith, Sue Davies, Francis Hodgson, Karen Hope, Rachael McLanaghan and Peter Ride; the staff of Photography Workshop/Portfolio Gallery, Edinburgh: Jane Brettle, Gloria Chalmers, Mary Ann Kennedy and Sally Rice; Kay Ritchie; Pam Scott; the Scottish Arts Council; Sarah Stevenson of the Scottish National Portrait Gallery; Graham and Joyce Smith; the staff and Board of Stills Gallery, Edinburgh, past and present, especially Jane Brettle, Gloria Chalmers, Gavin Jack and Rob Powell; Ian Swindale; the staff of Theatre Workshop, Edinburgh, especially Adrian Harris; on the technical side: the staff of Eastern Photocolour, Edinburgh, especially Frank Cornfield and Alex Porteous; the staff of Edinburgh Cameras, especially John Semple; and the staff of J. Lizars Ltd, Edinburgh, especially Norman Houston and Martin Baker.

I am also grateful to the Trustees of The Photographers' Trust Fund for their generous financial support of some of the work included in the book.

For their greatly valued support and friendship, often over many years and accompanied by generous hospitality, and for wide-ranging discussions during which ideas developed which were highly relevant to the content of the book, I should particularly like to thank: Donald, Aileen, David, Lucy and John Addison; Marion, Colin, Colin Ewan and Innes Campbell; Ann Brignall; Rosalind, Victor and Richard Lobb; Lyn Rogers and Peter Field; Peter and Catriona Savage; Gordon and Elspeth Strachan and members of the Sacred Geometry group; Geoff Pickup; Moira Stevenson and David Groome; Yvonne Taylor; and most especially Mahala Andrews and Maria, David, Martin and Timothy Chamberlain.

On the publishing side: Clare de Rouen of Zwemmers for help and advice; the staff of Aurum Press, past and present, especially Michael Alcock and Helen Torlesse for their faith in, and support of, the book through many vicissitudes, Mandy Greenfield for expert editing assistance, and Helen Lewis, Philip Gilderdale and Geoff Barlow for their sympathetic and excellent design and production expertise.

For his sensitive personal and particular response to the theme of the book, and for some most enjoyable discussions, Dominic Cooper.

Most of all, for his continuing involvement and support in every possible way, and for his equal part in the making of the photographs in his capacity as photographic pilot, operations manager and navigator, I should like to thank my husband, Angus Macdonald.

Although so many people have generously contributed to making this book possible, the opinions which it expresses, and any errors which it almost inevitably contains, are nevertheless my own responsibility.

Patricia Macdonald, April 1989